American Heroes

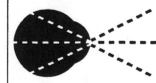

This Large Print Book carries the
Seal of Approval of N.A.V.H.

American Heroes

Their Lives, Their Values, Their Beliefs

Dr. Robert B. Pamplin, Jr.
and
Gary K. Eisler

Thorndike Press • Thorndike, Maine

Library of Congress Cataloging in Publication Data

Pamplin, Robert B., 1941–
    American heroes : their lives, their values, their beliefs /
Robert B. Pamplin, Jr. and Gary K. Eisler.
    p.   cm.
    ISBN 0-7862-0541-5 (lg. print : hc)
    1. Heroes — United States — Biography.
    2. Biography — 20th century. 3. United States — Biography.
    4. Large type books. I. Eisler, Gary K. II. Title.
    [CT220.P36 1995]
    920.073—dc20   95-35377

DEDICATION

Simply the nicest person I know, with a heart as generous and sun-warmed as old Georgia itself, my wife, Marilyn, is a hero in the purest sense.

ROBERT B. PAMPLIN, JR.

To my wife, Bonnie, whose courage and cheer during her struggle with cancer have been an inspiration to all who know her, and whose help and encouragement in the writing of this book were invaluable.

GARY K. EISLER

CONTENTS

Who Are Our Heroes Today?

"We can't all be heroes. Some of us have to stand on the curb and clap as they go by." Those are the words of Will Rogers, American humorist and actor from a past generation, who was known for his pithy wisdom.

We can picture exactly what he means: Battalions of brave young people in uniform, marching to the cadence of drums and bugles down a boulevard lined with flag-waving citizens. Apollo astronauts, back from a voyage to the moon, riding in convertibles through a blizzard of confetti. Sports stars waving to throngs of adoring fans.

For generations, that has been the image of the American hero. But this book was written to suggest that perhaps there is plenty of room in the spotlight of heroism for those of us who are not movie stars or astronauts. Perhaps we actually can do more than stand on the sidelines and cheer. Perhaps heroism today has less to do with magnificent deeds than with everyday life, our relations with our friends and families, and our service to our communities. Being a hero today, we suggest, means a life well-lived.

What does it mean to be a hero? We asked noted futurists and authors of *Office Biology: Why Tuesday Is the Most Productive Day and Other Relevant Facts for Survival in the Workplace*, Edith Weiner and Arnold Brown to offer their comments: "The dictionary has several definitions for the word hero," they write. "A great warrior; someone admired for achievements or noble qualities; a person of courage; an idol; a person honored by public worship; someone held to be of divine descent; an individual who displays fortitude in suffering and; perhaps most importantly, a mythological or legendary figure who is larger than life."

Americans are confused about heroes today, Weiner and Brown observe, but that was not always the case. In the past, they continue, a hero was "noble, honorable, brave, strong, and willing to sacrifice himself to defend his people and his country. For example, at the battle of Gettysburg, Colonel Joshua Chamberlain was a hero. An unwarlike man thrust into crucial eminence in that awful, brutal battle, he acted with extraordinary courage, determination, and leadership. There was no confusion about what he was: he was a hero

. . . someone who protected, who used his courage and strength as a shield for those less brave and less strong.

"The literature of the past is full of heroes. The play of children in the past was based on those heroes, and as the children grew up they aspired to become like those heroes, because it was believed that heroes were us writ large. They were what we would all want to be and what we might become.

"The aspiration to heroic stature still exists. The dreams of glory are still universal. The problem is that, just like everything else in our complex, turbulent, and rapidly changing world, it is so much more difficult to believe anymore."

Perhaps more than any other generation, American youth at the end of the century have been robbed of the traditional American hero — the sports figure, the war hero, the movie star, the political leader. They have seen their "heroes" toppled because of sexual misconduct, greed, and crime. These fallen heroes may or may not be as moral as heroes of generations past, but today the press stalks them like big-game trophies, waiting for a sign of vulnerability on which to pounce. "It sometimes seems that the media have a mission to both make and unmake heroes," note Weiner and Brown.

11

"It is as if they are children, constructing grand structures out of Lego blocks, only to tear them apart in a frenzy of destruction. But it is too easy to blame that solely on the media. If television shows and magazine articles and books telling the sordid little truths about heroes weren't avidly consumed, the media would stop producing them."

Understandably, most Americans are disillusioned — especially with national public figures. We have learned that just because a person is a celebrity does not mean that individual is to be admired.

Around the world, people expect their heroes to emulate their culture's social code, comments Helen Fisher, research associate in the anthropology department at Rutgers University. Fisher is also the author of such books as *Anatomy of Love: The History of Monogamy, Adultery and Divorce* and *The Sex Contract: The Evolution of Human Behavior*. In our culture, we esteem those who rise above their own self-interest to help others — even if the effort requires sacrifice on their part. We do not esteem those who climb over others for their own self-interest.

"We do not wish our heroes to win at our expense . . ." she writes. "Heroes are individuals who exemplify some part of the culture's moral code: they act the way we ought to act. . . . Anthropologists call a culture's value system its 'ideal' culture, as opposed to the 'real' culture, what people really do."

Who can be our heroes? Whose example is worth following? What standards can we apply to separate the celebrities from the heroes?

Motivation separates heroes from celebrities; heroes do not set out for fame and fortune. They do what they do because of strongly held beliefs and are willing to make personal sacrifices for what they hold important, whether other people, morality or God is their priority. They try to do the impossible — and the effort always takes physical or mental courage — and live by a strong moral code. Their lives are impressive, making others willing to follow their examples or to accept their advice and guidance.

In America, people are reexamining not only concepts of celebrity and heroism, but also of success. In the past, an individual who is good at accumulating wealth was considered successful. But if that's all there were to it, then we would not consider as successful those individuals who have spent lifetimes sacrificing their own comfort for the welfare of others. Mother Teresa, for example, has dedicated herself to providing solace to the downtrodden, and yet will leave this world with no accumulation of money. In actuality, success also comes from using one's talents for the welfare of others. In other words, a person of value who makes the world a better place is a bona fide success. By this definition, the heroes profiled in this book have led tremendously successful lives.

As a people, we have become very wise about distinguishing between the hero and the celebrity with a good press agent. But we also recognize that some celebrities are genuine heroes, though not all heroes are celebrities. Oprah Winfrey, for example, is both a hero and a celebrity. Our own parents, by and large, may be heroes but probably are not celebrities.

Bill Cosby, comedian, author, and one of the American heroes included in this book, says: "Forget about the celebrities. We're not gods; we're not perfect and we have our problems." Instead, Cosby points to hard-working parents as the best role models for children. "Tell me that your father who comes home and changes clothes to go to his second job to support you by working eighteen hours a day is not a positive image."

Matt McClanahan, a high school freshman in a Portland, Oregon suburb, agrees: "Superman's dead, Batman retired, and too many sports players will do anything for money or drugs," he wrote for a local newspaper. "Why not something attainable? I'd go for my dad. . . . He married once and is still married to my mom. He's a good, decent man who knows what society dishes out and won't have any part of it."

Most young Americans agree with him that their heroes are to be found among family members, friends, teachers, and others they can trust. Many young people admire the wisdom their parents have gained after long struggles to support their families.

The question is, are there people left with name recognition — people we are all familiar with — who are worthy of our admiration. We believe there are. *American Heroes* offers short biographies of some of them. We picked well-known names in the arts, business, entertainment, government, and sports. We chose men and women, young and old, from a variety of religions, races, and national origins.

This is a book aimed not at exploiting the reputations of the famous, but at illustrating valuable lessons to be learned through their lives. They were selected not for what you know about them, but for what you may not have known about them — that they have faced the same challenges many of us have faced: cancer, chronic illness, Down syndrome, sexism, sex abuse, sexual temptation, drug addiction, adoption, rejection, ignorance, prejudice, racism, poverty, wealth, war.

Each of our heroes not only successfully met his or her challenge, but then went on to help or inspire other people in their own life struggles. The individuals profiled in *American Heroes* are not to be worshipped, but to be studied and considered. Their inclusion is not for their honor but for our benefit.

To explore the concept of heroism, we conducted a national survey of hundreds of Americans in all age groups in every part of the country. We interviewed these individuals at length about what they considered to be heroic qualities, and we asked them to rank those attributes in importance. We also asked other questions about our society today.

The outcome is a snapshot of American values. The results may be surprising — in some cases alarming and in others encouraging. This is the only such widely-based survey that was privately sponsored — it was not a media survey. We offer a synthesis of the study in the next chapter, and survey specifics and resulting data in the Appendix.

One of the things we learned through the survey is how desperately our young people yearn for good role models. Ninety percent of the teenagers we surveyed agree that we need more heroes and heroines. Is this an especially unheroic era? Not according to Weiner and Brown. "The truth is, even the legendary heroes of Greek mythology were insufficient in number. It did, after all, take the Greeks ten years to defeat the Trojans. And the hero may be one particularly because heroism is rare."

In our study of American heroes, we have found some characteristics common throughout the centuries. Perhaps most important, our greatest heroes have had humble hearts.

George Washington, as commander in chief of the Continental Army, led his ragged band of patriots to victory over the British and on to American independence. He was a person well-known for his character and sense of justice, and when a grateful country offered to make him king, he declined and worked instead to build the greatest and longest-lasting democracy the world has seen.

When economic and political divisions led the American people to war against itself, Robert E. Lee reluctantly stepped forward to lead the forces of the South. His brilliance as a general was overshadowed by his compassion for his men. He lived by the principles of life that shaped the Southern gentleman: a genteel expression of caring, understanding, a conservative manner, and an unswerving belief in God.

Rather than see his men and the people of the Confederacy uselessly suffer, he shouldered the burden of surrendering the Southern dream of independence. Yet at his death, the whole nation mourned because of his humility and his exemplary life of service to God, country, and his fellow man.

More contemporary heroes have also been able to inspire and energize others. Jimmy Doolittle, to name one, straightened the backs of his countrymen at perhaps America's darkest hour. Following the Japanese attack on Pearl Harbor in December, 1941 and a string of humiliating losses after that, American morale was at a low ebb. But legendary aviator Doolittle used his ingenuity to launch cumbersome bombers from the decks of primitive aircraft carriers. He led a dangerous and unprecedented air raid over Japan only four months after the war began. His bravery showed that we could strike back, and he galvanized the American spirit to summon the will to victory.

On the home front, other heroes did their part to keep morale high. From 1944 to 1953, Lavonne Paire-Davis, known as "Pepper" Davis to baseball fans, was a star player in the All-American Girls Professional Baseball

League, which kept baseball alive during the war. (Paire-Davis was portrayed by Geena Davis in *A League of Their Own*, the movie that tells the story of the league.) "We played every night of the week and double-headers on Sundays and holidays, and traveled with no days off for travel," she recalls.

Paire-Davis was known as the "Queen of Diamonds" because she led all catchers in the league; she also played shortstop and third base. Though she was often injured, "Pepper" rarely came out of a game. In fact, she once broke a finger on her throwing hand during a play, and made a splint out of two Popsicle sticks so she could get back in the game.

Recently, although not in a time of emergency, baseball called her to service again. At seventy, Paire-Davis became chief spokesperson for the Women's National Adult Baseball Association, touring forty cities in nine weeks to promote the new league, which is open to all women between the ages of eighteen and sixty-five and has divisions for both experienced and amateur players. If she could, she'd love to play again herself after she recovers from knee surgery.

There will always be enough danger somewhere in the world to give rise to heroes who demonstrate physical courage and take action. One of the best examples is John Rys-Davies, an actor who, coincidentally, is best known for his roles in adventure films such as *Raiders of the Lost Ark*, *Indiana Jones and the Last Crusade*, and *War and Remembrance*; he was given the opportunity to live out the drama and excitement usually confined to his movie roles. Davies' son Tom, an ambitious photojournalist, traveled to Yugoslavia at the beginning of that country's civil war to try to capture the one photograph that would characterize the conflict. But he became emotionally involved in the struggle, and lost his objectivity, taking up a gun to fight on the side of the Croatians.

What was his father to do? Let his grown son make his own mistakes and live by them, or try to save the young man from his own indiscretion?

Davies decided to jump on the next flight to the Balkans. He flew to Yugoslavia to find his boy, and on Christmas morning he was in the middle of a war zone with sniper bullets ricocheting off burned-out buildings and incoming mortar shells blasting craters in the streets.

After a day of fruitlessly questioning partisans, the elder Davies returned to his hotel room Christmas night. That's when Tom called. Davies calmly told his son he planned to join the fight for Croatia and was on his way to Dubrovnik for his assignment, leaving Tom with his own questions. Was his father bluffing, or had he led the man into a dangerous and potentially suicidal mission? The son decided his own commitment could not become the reason to place his father in danger. Tom boarded a plane with his dad and returned home. Was it a performance, or would Davies have fought to save his son? "I'm glad we didn't have to find out," he said.

Davies' willingness to take action and face danger potentially saved the life of his son. But with another family, it was the loss of their son that elicited from them the compassion and generosity that captured the heart of a nation.

Nicholas Green was seven years old in 1994 when his parents took him to Italy on vacation. Although there is a high level of violence and highway robbery in Italy — among the worst in all of Europe — the family never dreamed that they would be overtaken by highway bandits as they drove their tiny rented car in a remote southern area. Masked men shot at their car several times.

When the gunmen gave up, the boy's father pulled over. He and his wife saw that one of their three children had been shot in the head, and two days later Nicholas was pronounced dead in a Messina hospital.

Instead of showing rage and calling for vengeance, the parents consistently said Italians were not to blame. Rather than saying they wanted nothing more to do with Italy, they donated the boy's organs to Italian children and said the gift would lessen their own pain.

"I would have liked him to live a long time," Nicholas's mother said. "Now I wish the same thing for his heart." That organ went to a fourteen-year-old Roman boy, Nicholas's liver to a nineteen-year-old Sicilian woman, one of his kidneys to a fourteen-year-old Puglia girl, and the other to an eleven-year-old Sicilian boy; his pancreas and eyes went to other Italian children.

Nicholas's parents' gesture hit Italy like a moral bomb. Especially since the country is not noted for its willingness to offer organs for transplant, the public was stunned by the Green's altruism after their son's tragic death. There was a national outpouring of sympathy for the parents, who were received by the president and the prime minister of Italy, given a gold medal by the mayor of Rome, and flown home by the Italian air force.

Although a child died in Italy, because of the family's compassion, the boy lives on. In addition to the individual lives saved by the organ transplants, a city named a street after Nicholas. The spirit of the country was challenged to change as newspapers decried the lawlessness. The killers turned themselves in. Many Italians called the Green family and said they were ashamed of their country, but Nicholas's father replied, "I believe I've never loved Italy as much as I do now."

Giving from his own body so that others might live made Nicholas Green a posthumous hero. Yet many others heroically fight disability every day in order to live, inspiring others as a result. George Mendoza, who lost eighty percent of his sight when he was fifteen years old, is one example.

Despite his physical limitation, Mendoza went on to become a world-class runner, representing the United States in the 1980 Olympics for the Physically Disabled in Holland and the 1984 International Games for the Disabled in New York. His life story was chronicled in a television documentary, "Running Toward the Light," and he has been profiled in many magazines. By speaking to groups of young people and the disabled, he has done so much to help others overcome their physical challenges that New Mexico, where he lives, has made October 1 "George Mendoza Day."

The heroes in this book are known for their compassion. Their great achievements could easily have led, instead, to pride, and pride comes before destruction. "Beware that you brag about standing, lest you fall," warns Johnny Cash, who is among them. Pride also causes us to devalue others, in extreme cases, to destroying them.

Religious convictions also help control pride. As hero Elizabeth Dole says, "I think I can face challenging situations and feel there's a source of strength beyond myself, that it's not all just on my shoulders." Faith in God keeps even the most successful people humble, because they realize that by themselves they can do nothing.

Which brings us to another quality of the American hero: their tragic dimension. Many of the subjects profiled survived situations that could have crushed them. It's said that heroes overcome adversity. But more than merely overcoming an obstacle, heroes have used their adversity as the very thing that defines and enables their brave acts. Heroic potential, it seems, requires challenge, adversity, even tragedy for fulfillment.

Oprah Winfrey, who had been sexually abused when she was a child, fought back as an adult by sponsoring a law to protect children in the future. Betty Ford, whose life could have been swallowed up by breast cancer and substance abuse, instead created a new life helping other women in their struggle against these diseases. Elie Wiesel survived a

Nazi death camp and became an advocate for compassion and kindness. For many of them, their compassion for others was born out of great misfortune. According to former President Jimmy Carter, "There are people just as good as we are, just not as lucky."

One thing is true about all our heroes: they believe in making the most of what they have. Chris Burke's family certainly did not bargain for a child with Down syndrome, but they went forward and raised their child without complaint. Antonia Coello Novello would have happily started her life without a birth defect, but she did the best she could with what she had.

But great adversity also raises questions. What's the difference between the individual who is crushed by troubles and the one who rises to the challenge? Why does a long ordeal make some people kind and wise, while others come out mean and bitter? Is it strictly a matter of character? Are some people simply stronger than others? Are there golden threads that link heroic lives?

The link we found among all of the heroes we studied is the support our heroes enjoyed early in their lives. They all were connected to people who believed in them. For many, but not all, that support came from family members or friends.

25

Jackie Joyner-Kersee, for example, was blessed with a grandmother who believed so much in her that the she gave the baby a name, Jacqueline, after Jacqueline Kennedy, that would remind her every day of her great potential. And with the expectations for success carried within her name, Jackie Joyner-Kersee became, perhaps, the greatest athlete in history.

The lesson for the rest of us is to find the support we need to live our lives — and to be that support for others. To expand on Will Rogers' observation, maybe we all should be marching in the parade and clapping for others at the same time.

Other heroes were inspired by no one they knew, but by a role model left behind. When John Rollins was a boy struggling with the poverty of the Great Depression, his mother read him success stories from Horatio Alger. From those stories, Rollins gained an expectation that he could accomplish great things. He ultimately founded several companies that employ thousands of people and earn hundreds of millions of dollars. And he helps young people learn they can successfully meet their own goals.

Dave Thomas of Wendy's had a stepfather who told him he would never amount to anything, but he refused to accept that verdict, and instead went out and found his own role model. There is an art to picking role models, he believes; his advice appears in the chapter beginning on page 255.

"Ultimately, perhaps, heroism cannot be defined except by example," write Weiner and Brown. "So we look to the lives and deeds of an individual and say 'Yes, this was a hero,' or 'No, this was not.' And that is why a book such as this one can be so useful. The lives of our heroes can both entertain and educate us: we learn heroism from what they were and what they did; we cheer or cry as their stories move us and thrill us. They can make us want to become better. They can tell us what to measure ourselves — and others — by.

"We are moving into a brand new world. As we start a new century, a new millennium, we may be making as radical a break with the past as the one that marked the transition to the Industrial Revolution. Much of what we know will seem not just outdated but antiquated. Many, perhaps most, of the structures and systems of today may be useless tomorrow.

"But there are eternal values. As we embark on this uncharted new sea, these values can be our oars and our compass. Among them will be heroism. We will still need heroes;

27

perhaps we will need them more — to protect us as we go into the unknown. . . .

"It may be that our new heroes will appear to be very different from those of the past: reformers rather than warriors, inventors rather than explorers. But very likely they will still display those attributes of courage, determination, nobility of character and purpose, and compassion for others that have always inspired us.

"In many parts of the world physical strength and the prowess of the warrior will still be the primary attributes of the hero. But for much of the world, the new information-based world, we are likely to see new kinds of heroes as well — smart, clever, innovative people, the new Daniel Boones. And it may be that we will increasingly find our heroes among us rather than above us, and that may not be a bad thing at all."

Synthesis of Survey Results

Young people are saying: "Give us heroes to look up to. We don't care if they're famous. We don't care if they're brave or strong. Just so long as they are honest, have high moral standards, and are compassionate."

How do we know?

We asked them, as well as hundreds of other Americans, in what is believed to be the country's first nonmedia-originated national survey on heroism and ethics.

If you thought being famous or physically gifted or even brave would put you at the top, you're out of step with most Americans today. Those qualities were at the bottom of their list of what makes a hero.

Honesty, followed closely by being compassionate and having high moral standards are what most Americans think is most important in a hero. This causes us to conclude that their views have been profoundly shaped by recent scandals involving celebrities and national figures.

We commissioned the survey of American views of heroism and ethics because we wanted *American Heroes* to offer the most comprehensive view possible about what people feel are the qualities of a hero, and what, if anything, would disqualify someone from being a hero.

The results guided our selection of who was featured in this book. The people profiled in the book illustrate one or more of these virtues. We asked some of the profiled individuals to comment on the findings, and those interviews are included in this chapter.

Noted Rutgers University anthropologist Helen Fisher remarks, "Heroes are individuals who exemplify some part of the culture's moral code; they act the way we ought to act. So when these authors asked 950 American men, women, and teenagers what constituted a hero, they actually elicited from these informants contemporary American values." In other words, we wound up with a snapshot of today's mores.

"Give a one to ten rating for this series of issues presumed important in considering someone a hero or heroine." That was one of the questions people all over the country were asked by telephone. Below are comments on some of the responses.

HONESTY

The highest rated issue, honesty was considered tops by over eighty-three percent of respondents. Noted futurists Edith Weiner and Arnold Brown are interested by the emphasis placed on honesty. "What is striking, when we look at the survey done for this book, is that the number-one attribute for heroism, according to survey respondents, is honesty. Correspondingly, the number-one characteristic that disqualifies a person from being a hero is dishonesty. We doubt very much that, had such a survey been done in past years, honesty would have ranked so high. Why honesty? Is it because people have become skeptical of what passes for heroism these days?"

Agreeing that honesty holds a remarkable place in American concerns today is anthropologist Fisher. "Americans admire honesty so much that we tell the truth even when it hurts our loved ones and disrupts daily life," she writes. "Honesty is central to our moral code. And the results of the survey parrot this American ideal. Deceit heads the list of qualities that these informants say would disqualify a person from heroic status. This response reflects our American moral code. But these informants all found being selfish and performing acts for personal gain repugnant too."

One of the interesting things we found was how differently from the general population teenagers see things. Our survey clearly shows a division between generations when it comes to honesty. Although young people said they admire honesty more than any other virtue, it is noteworthy how far their survey responses about specific questions of honesty varied from the norm. A significant number of teenagers said they would be willing to cheat on a test if they wouldn't get caught. Their intentions are strong, but they are nonetheless still weak and know they might slip.

This may be one reason they also feel the need for role models — to be assured it's possible to lead an honest life. Chris Burke identifies the significance of role models, particularly those found among the family: "Young children need to be taught that family is the most important value in life. Then, as they grow older, they will have respect for themselves and their way of life. Then, they can teach their children, in time, the important values of life. We should be certain to teach children to be aware of others, then they will learn to accept everyone."

It is possibly another reason why teenagers, like the rest of the population, overwhelmingly agreed that one can still be considered a hero or heroine if they've ever done "anything bad." They want to be heroes, but know it's impossible to lead a perfect life.

For teenagers, six other qualities were more important than having high moral standards — such as having strong beliefs, willingness to do the right thing, willingness to sacrifice, willingness to stand by principles and willingness to risk one's own life. After honesty, teenagers ranked as most important the determination to overcome obstacles, and then being willing to do the right thing no matter what the circumstances. The general population had rated being compassionate and having high moral standards higher.

It's also interesting how differently than teenage girls teenage boys see life. For example, it was more important to teenage girls to be honest, to stand by principles, to have high moral standards, and to be compassionate than for boys. To teenage boys, on the other hand, overcoming obstacles was the only quality they rated higher than did the teenage girls. And teenage boys were more than twice as likely as were teenage girls to agree with the statement that "under certain circumstances, violence is appropriate."

The widest spread between teenagers' answers was in having an optimistic attitude —

girls were more than twice as likely to rate this as important. Could this be because girls are more likely to become depressed?

We asked people what would disqualify someone from heroic status. The most common answer was being dishonest or deceitful — offered almost twice as often as the next choice, which was being selfish and using others.

COMPASSION

"Given the social . . . orientation of teenagers, I am not surprised that fewer teens in this survey regarded compassion as an important aspect of a hero . . . ," comments Fisher. "Why should teens express compassion for the larger social group unless this energy expenditure reaps reproductive benefits for them?

"Teenage girls, however, rated 'being compassionate' higher than did teenage boys. This feminine regard for compassion may come from women's ancestral tradition of bearing and rearing young. Compassion is, and always has been, essential to successful motherhood. Moreover, a wealth of psychological data indicates that girls and women naturally cast themselves in a web of ties and obligations, then they nurture these networks. Compassion probably enabled ancestral women to maintain this essential network, leaving this respect for compassion in young (as well as aging) women today."

FAME

Some characteristics were less important than we might have expected. "It may be significant," Fisher writes, "that the lowest ranking attribute in the survey is being famous. Perhaps people are not misled by the modern media confusion between heroism and celebrity."

Agreeing is Johnny Cash: "Fame is the least important quality in being a hero. It's personal sacrifice for the good of others that makes a hero."

WILLING TO RISK LIFE

"I am not surprised that males aged nineteen to twenty-four rated 'being willing to risk your life' much higher than other respondents did," Fisher observes. "Or that boys more regularly thought that violence was appropriate under certain circumstances. Young men have high levels of testosterone; they are at the peak age for aggressive, daring interactions."

COURAGE

Weiner and Brown observe another shift in thinking: "The survey results do show some confusion concerning what has always been considered one of the primary attributes of the hero — courage. Being courageous ranks fourth from the bottom in the list of seventeen attributes. Yet specific aspects of being courageous — willingness to do the right thing, willingness to stand by principles, willingness to risk one's life — rank much higher.

"Perhaps the confusion is over what courage means. At a time when we label as heroes people who were taken hostage and were rescued by the efforts of others, that kind of confusion is inevitable. . . . Perhaps that is because, at a time when we feel helpless in the strong winds of change, we identify more with victims than we do with heroes. That may also be why the media tend to glorify ordinary acts of civic virtue — e.g., a feature article exalting a homeowner who recycles."

IT IS IMPORTANT TO HAVE A SPIRITUAL LIFE

It is informative how differently various

36

parts of the country feel about certain issues. In the Agreement Statements, the issue receiving the most agreement was "It's important to have a spiritual life," to which eighty-seven percent of the sample agreed.

But ninety-eight percent of respondents in the North Central region (Wisconsin, Illinois, Indiana, Michigan, and Ohio) agreed. The statement also got strong support from females in the twenty-five-to-forty-nine age group and those over sixty-five.

Johnny Cash was asked what we should be doing to educate our young people about values. To Cash, the teaching goes in the other direction. "I've been trying to learn from young people," he says. "I ask young people — my children — about my own decisions. They sometimes ask my opinion and I sometimes ask theirs. You'll get honest, straightforward answers and it builds their sense of self-esteem and importance.

"Honesty and love of family are fundamental values, but a lot of young people don't have families, so they get their values from people they admire.

"Church is important, but believing in the goodness of God is more important. Faith and communication with God are what's important in worship. Church is very necessary because it gives regimentation and rules, and most of us need to be told what is right and wrong."

THE MEDIA MAKES HEROES OUT OF PEOPLE WHO DON'T DESERVE IT

Americans see behind the glitz and glamour the media puffs up around their celebrities, and see famous people as no better than they are themselves. Sometimes they are worse. This is why so many Americans look away from the spotlight for their heroes — to people they know. Chris Burke says, "I think we need both education and entertainment, but it is very important that each should be done in a responsible way."

Johnny Cash urges Americans to take greater control over the input they receive from the media. "Occasionally a good show comes along like 'Dr. Quinn, Medicine Woman,' with its high moral, spiritual, and family values. But there is so much hype on television, so much done for ratings that it bothers me.

"There is a lot of good material in books in the library. Great classics and new books such as *The Shipping News* take me on a better flight of fancy than television. Those who don't read have no advantage over those who can't."

WE NEED MORE HEROES AND HEROINES

As an Agreement Statement, this one got the nod from eighty percent of the respondents overall, and it ranked sixth in priority. But from teenagers it got ninety percent agreement, and was at the top of their list. Our young people are telling us they want good role models, people to look up to and inspire them.

This raises such questions as what is the most important value or theme we should be trying to teach our young people, or whether they should be teaching us. Johnny Cash said: "I don't think teenagers have less moral values. They are more honest."

HEROISM ISN'T ANY ONE ACT

Eighty-four percent of the general population now sees heroism as a way of life, rather than a single act or deed. For teenagers, the percent of agreement was even higher — eighty-nine percent.

Weiner and Brown remark: "What is encouraging about the survey is the high level of agreement that heroism is a way of life, not merely a single act. This indicates an understanding, not yet destroyed, of what being a hero has always meant. This same understanding is implicit in the high level of agreement that being a hero entails having a spiritual life. Heroism is indeed more than deeds. It can encompass deeds, but those deeds arise as much out of the character of the hero as they do out of the circumstances into which the hero is put."

MARRIAGE IS A DYING INSTITUTION

"This survey is a trove of American attitudes . . . ," declares Fisher. "But there is one I would like to counter; it does not reflect our culture or our nature. Two out of five respondents (thirty-nine percent) believed that 'marriage is a dying institution.' Indeed, over forty-six percent of today's marriages are likely to end in divorce. But these data do not suggest that marriage is a dying institution.

"On the contrary, some ninety-five percent of Americans still marry by age forty-nine. And of those who do divorce, about eighty percent of men and seventy-five percent of women remarry.

"Moreover, marriage is a cultural universal. The vast majority of men and women in every culture wed, a human penchant that is not likely to change. . . . So although the family changes with changing times, it will always survive. We are built to love and rear our children as a team."

UNDER CERTAIN CIRCUMSTANCES, VIOLENCE IS APPROPRIATE

The boys loved this statement: sixty-five percent of boys aged fifteen to eighteen agreed, compared to twenty-seven percent of girls. The proportion of males who agreed dropped drastically in the nineteen-to-twenty-four age group — down to forty-six percent. Could this be because they are of age for military service, or have they already witnessed too much suffering because of bloodshed among young people?

HYPOTHETICAL QUESTIONS

Respondents were asked to answer these questions. Each question, in one way or another, has to do with honesty. Our findings show that Americans believe honesty is important, despite the personal cost.
- "If you found a wallet in the street with
  $5,000 in it, would you turn it in?"

Three out of four teenagers said they would return the wallet. Among older adults, nine out of ten said they would. The positive response to this question, from both young and old alike, was surprising. Add to this the finding that honesty was rated the most important virtue for every generation, and we get a picture of an American people who are far more honest than they are sometimes given credit for.

Johnny Cash says of the results: "Teens may be more honest than adults. I think teens would be more likely to give [the wallet] back." Adults may have been more willing to keep the money, but not as likely to admit it as teens, who have not yet learned the art of hypocrisy.

Helen Fisher finds the responses to these hypothetical questions the most interesting part of the survey. She observes that if the survey indicates that slightly more adults would return the hypothetical wallet stuffed with cash, it's to their "advantage to support the prevailing moral codes and thus strengthen the fabric of the culture. If society survives, their children will benefit from their altruism."

- "If you banged someone's car in a parking lot — but no one saw you — would you turn yourself in?"

If your car were banged in a parking lot by an adult, one in ten would not tell about it. But if your car were damaged by a fifteen-to-eighteen year-old, it's almost three times as likely that you would not learn about it via the driver.

The survey revealed that eighty-five percent of respondents said they would turn themselves in if they'd banged someone's car in a parking lot and no one saw them, ten percent said they would not, and five percent were unsure. The results suggest that most people understand that honesty may not have an immediate reward but has the potential of a long-term benefit.

Fisher says, "Perhaps individuals maintain high moral standards in all situations because a few of these circumstances will have such high benefits that these perquisites far exceed the losses incurred by all other altruistic acts."

- "If your best friend were doing something illegal, would you turn him in?"

The response to this was split — forty-one percent said they would, forty-two percent said they wouldn't, and seventeen percent did not know.

But only thirty-three percent of teenagers would turn in their best friend — sixty percent said they would not. Teenagers were less ambivalent about the decision. Only seven percent said they didn't know what they would do, compared to seventeen percent of the general population.

"It's no surprise that teens were the least likely to turn in a friend who was doing something illegal," Fisher comments. "Teens often (and perhaps naturally) regard it as immoral to abandon a member of the peer group.

"Human moral codes shift with age. Children are exceedingly self-centered; this is appropriate behavior for individuals struggling through the most vulnerable period of their lives. Teenage morality centers around the peer group instead. . . . Teens needed to make strong social bonds with peers, ties they would depend on to survive throughout their lives. Then as one ages, one's moral system expands to include more and more of the community. Older people have already reproduced. So if they support the norms of the society, the culture may survive — and their children may flourish too. Teenage morality and the moral reasoning of older Americans are both evident in this survey."

- "If you knew one of your parents were cheating, would you tell the other parent?"

The younger the respondent, the more likely they were to tell. Overall, forty-five percent of respondents would tell the other parent, forty-three percent would not, and twelve percent did not know. But with nineteen-to-twenty-four-year-olds, sixty-four percent said they would tell the other parent. That figure drops to fifty percent for those twenty-five to thirty-four, and thirty-nine percent for those thirty-five to forty-nine.

- "If you knew one of your close relatives were cheating, would you tell his or her spouse?"

The question was asked of people forty-five and older, and only twenty-two percent said they would tell if they knew someone were cheating. Sixty-two percent said they would not and seventeen percent didn't know. Could this come from a desire to remain uninvolved, or from many years of experience in relationships?

- "Would you be unfaithful if you knew you wouldn't get caught?"

Young males are by far the most likely to answer yes to being unfaithful if they wouldn't get caught. They were three times more likely than the average to say they would.

Of the total cross-section, seven percent of both men and women said they would cheat on their spouses if they wouldn't get caught. That is an amazingly low percentage, and indicates that despite a relatively high divorce rate, Americans still believe in marital fidelity. Even among males aged nineteen to twenty-two, fully seventy-eight percent said they would not commit adultery if they wouldn't get caught.

- "Would you cheat on a school test if you would get a better grade and not get caught?"

Most teenagers — fifty-nine percent — said they would not cheat on a school test while forty percent admitted they would. The split was forty-five percent of boys and thirty-seven percent of girls saying they would cheat. Those who would cheat are willing to compromise their own sense of honesty for the sake of getting ahead. Ironically, they believe it is the people who have built the habit of honesty who are most likely to win trust and are therefore likely to advance further than the dishonest.

"Teenagers were also more likely to feel that lying was OK under certain circumstances," Fisher observes. "In fact, forty percent of teens would cheat on a school test if they knew they wouldn't get caught. These people clearly acknowledge the expediency of cheating. Teens, it appears, are less saturated by American moral codes. . . . (Perhaps these teens also gave more honest answers in this survey because they are less skilled at deception — and self-deception.)"

- "If your friends wanted you to do

something that you knew was wrong
— but it made you popular — would
you do it?"

Eighty-nine percent said they wouldn't, while nine percent said they would with two percent not sure. But the sex split is informative: seventeen percent of boys said they would, while only three percent of girls said they would.

ABOUT THE SURVEY

William Angell of Angell & Company conducted the survey. This Westport, Connecticut firm prepares proprietary and confidential national and international surveys for private organizations and major corporations. His is one of the most highly respected survey firms in the country and this is perhaps the only privately sponsored study of these topics in which teenagers' responses are presented separately from adults. A total of eight hundred cross-section interviews were completed.

Most such studies are conducted by television stations, newspapers, or magazines. When surveys are of a publication's readership, the value of the responses can be limited because the polling is often restricted to the readership. We decided against a mail poll, because the results are limited to those people who choose to send back their replies. Taking a survey in person would mean many areas would be too remote to be reached.

Although no survey is perfect, our national probability sample comes as close as possible to accurately reflecting the public mood. We used a computer to randomly select telephone numbers, which allowed us to also reach people whose numbers are unlisted. We screened subjects on the telephone to learn their age and sex and whether they were employed in market research, which would have disqualified them. Subjects were assured of their anonymity to ensure their answers would be candid. Full study details appear in the Appendix of this book.

Chris Burke

When Christopher Joseph Burke was born on August 26, 1965, there were no television series such as "Life Goes On." In the show, Corky Thacher, the character played by Burke, has Down syndrome. He is nonetheless portrayed living a productive life full of the very same joys and problems the rest of us face.

But the scenario is not a fantasy limited only to a television screen. Burke has realized it almost exactly in real life. He has become wealthy in his own right as the star of a television series. He has become a spokesperson for everyone with Down syndrome. But his success is most significant because it has given countless other people with disabilities the chance to fulfill their potential.

Thirty years ago, when Burke was born, there was another word for people with Down syndrome: mongoloids. The term was coined by John Langdon Down, a London doctor and cousin to Charles Darwin who, in 1866, was the first to classify various kinds of mental retardation. He chose the term because the symptoms of the syndrome — shortness, slanted eyes, and flat faces — were evocative of some Asian peoples.

Thirty years ago, parents were routinely advised to put afflicted children in institutions — to get rid of them as soon as possible because they had no future. Back then, most states routinely sterilized children born with the disorder. In fact, as much as three years after Burke was born, in an article in *The Atlantic Monthly*, a respected theologian advocated immediate euthanasia for all children born with Down syndrome.

Burke's parents can look back at his birthday with the perspective of those who made a difficult choice in the face of adversity only to later have the correctness of their decision affirmed. After only six hours of labor at St. Vincent Hospital in Manhattan, Burke's mother, Marian, delivered her fourth child, "the cutest baby in existence." The fact that she was thirty-nine years old and that eleven years had passed since her last child was born made the baby's arrival that much more thrilling.

But her doctor was not equally joyful. She drew Marian's attention to the folds of skin over the baby's eyes. "They're slanted," the doctor said. "The nurses noticed it first. The baby is a mongoloid, Marian. He will probably never walk or talk. He won't amount to anything. Put him in an institution," the doctor advised her. "Forget you ever had him. It will be the best thing for you and your family."

For Frank and Marian Burke, the news that their baby was a mongoloid was practically a death sentence. At the time, only eighty percent of infants born with Down syndrome would live past their first birthdays; the average life expectancy was twelve years. Their weakened immune systems lead to a high incidence of pneumonia. They develop leukemia at a rate fifteen to thirty times higher than other children. They suffer from Alzheimer's disease more commonly than do other people. And the incomplete brain development characteristic of the condition is the most prevalent cause of mental retardation. With a few exceptions, nearly every child born with Down syndrome — five thousand are born each year in the United States to families of every ethnic and socioeconomic group — has less mental capacity than a normal child.

The reason Chris Burke did not fall into an institutional abyss is that his family would not allow it. The Burkes were accustomed to adversity and heartache, and had faith they would overcome this new challenge. They simply refused to give up on their son.

Frank Burke had been shot down over Germany during World War II when he was a gunner in a bomber. He spent a year as a prisoner of the Nazis in Stalag 17 and endured hunger, cold, and a forced march through the snow before he was liberated. When that day finally came, the twenty-year-old already understood that life was fragile and that he had been spared — when so many others were taken — for some reason. "I realized you must be thankful for life and play the hand you were dealt," he remembers.

Marian Brady and Frank Burke were married on October 2, 1948, in a Catholic church in New York. Their first three children were born over the next six years. The family made it a point to celebrate not the day Frank was liberated, but April 8, the day he was shot down. It was their way of turning misfortune on its head, a skill that would serve them well. "If something didn't go the way we wanted, the first chance we had we would go out and celebrate," Marian Burke has said. "It was our way of saying, 'We'll work it out. We'll make the best of it.' It helped us get back on track and feel better about it."

Even before their youngest son was born, the Burkes had called upon their resilience to deal with many misfortunes. Marian's mother,

Helen, died suddenly of a burst gall bladder while waiting to see an emergency-room doctor. The Burkes' second child developed polio — although it proved to be a mild case. And Marian's brother had just married when his new wife fell ill with cancer. While her sister-in-law was convalescing, her brother contracted cancer himself, and died nine months before his wife.

Despite all this, learning that her new baby had no future was "the worst moment of my entire life," Marian Burke recalls. Yet she and her husband didn't for a moment entertain the idea of putting their baby away. "He was mine and I was going to take him home no matter what," she says. They explained the situation to the children, who took it well.

"The fact that Chris had Down syndrome meant nothing to them. I told them that all we needed was to work together with him. From that time on, it was as if he had five parents, not two," Burke's mother describes. His siblings were old enough not to mind the extra attention Burke got, and were not particularly concerned about his differences. They took pride in their brother and, even when others shied away, never hid him or were ashamed of him. In fact, the siblings competed to see who could teach him the most.

He was so cute, his older sisters, Emily and Anne, and brother, Francis Dewey (nicknamed J.R.), played with him and read to him constantly, stimulating Burke's development. Everyone in the family made it a personal goal to help make Burke as normal as possible. As a result, his development was not much slower than normal. He began talking at eighteen months and walked at about two years.

(Studies would later prove that children who were raised by their families fared better in life than did institutionalized children, ranking higher on every standardized mental, physical, and social test. Today, only about ten percent of children with Down syndrome are institutionalized; instead, most are enrolled in intervention programs within a few weeks of birth.)

Nor were the relationships one-sided. Those who gave to Burke found that they received much in return. Frank Burke, at the time a New York City police officer, observes that his youngest son " . . . taught the kids that everyone is going to have adversity, but you have to rise above it. I know it drew our family together," he recalls.

The Burkes found that the ongoing crisis they were experiencing together gave them a sense of fellowship with other people. "Chris brought out a benevolent spirit in us all," his father says. "We grew to have more sensitivity for others. It brought us out of our narrow, rigid view of the world. And it changed my attitude about a whole range of people. . . ."

Perhaps most importantly, the Burkes decided what their approach to this situation would be. "We tried to get up and get on with life, not let this burden us," Frank Burke says. "As during the war, I took the attitude that these were the cards we were dealt, this was the hand we would play."

One of the ways they played those cards was to take their son to a speech therapist. Although Burke, like most children with Down syndrome, had difficulty speaking because his mouth is small and his tongue and facial muscles underdeveloped, working with the therapist enabled him to compensate. He would sing along with "Sesame Street" and imitate the characters; he loved to perform for the family.

As his older siblings left the nest, Burke's parents feared loneliness for him. They decided to enroll him in the Kennedy Child Study Center, an outgrowth of the Kennedy family's many efforts to help children with mental disabilities reach their maximum potential through early education and treatment. At first Burke went to the center twice a week; by the age of five, he was going to full-day classes. Above average in learning ability compared to other children in the center, at eight he graduated in a cap and gown ceremony.

Even though some children with Down syndrome were by now being "mainstreamed" in public schools, Burke's parents decided to keep him out. He attended two boarding schools, the Cardinal Cushing School and Training Center near Boston, and Don Guanella, in Springfield, Pennsylvania.

His mother sometimes allowed herself to wonder what might have become of her son had he not had Down syndrome. "I think he would have been someone really important. I think he would have had an impact in the world," she thought.

But as far as Burke was concerned, he never accepted that he could not do what he wanted, refusing to believe anyone who said otherwise. He wanted to be an actor, and that's what he was going to do.

His choice didn't come as much of a surprise to his parents. As a child, Burke loved watching "Little House on the Prairie," "Growing Pains," and "The Brady Bunch" on television. At first his family feared his television habit might lead him to become more inactive in later years, possibly preventing him from becoming a productive adult. But he was far from a passive audience. Burke taped his favorite movies and watched them over and over, memorizing the words. As he entered adolescence, he often wrote story ideas for television shows. He became obsessed with entertainment.

"I have wanted to be an actor ever since I was a little munchkin, when I was five years old," Burke wrote in his autobiography, *A Special Kind of Hero*. "When I told people what I wanted to do, they didn't think it would happen. But I always thought it could. I believed in my dreams," Burke says.

"There is no doubt that I wanted to become a big Hollywood star. I also wanted to help handicapped people. I wanted to show everyone that people with handicaps can be responsible. I wanted everyone to see that people with Down syndrome can do a job just like them. We have feelings and interests and we want to do our very best."

In late 1986 Burke got his opportunity. Michael Braverman, a writer and producer, had a script idea that Warner Brothers wanted to produce into a series for ABC. Called "Desperate," it had a part for someone with Down syndrome. Auditions were held in New York and Los Angeles, and the mother of a boy who was too young for the part knew Burke and recommended the casting agent call him.

Burke was overjoyed at the opportunity,

and went in for the audition taping. He read lines and talked about himself — especially his ambition to become an actor. When Braverman saw the tape and realized how well Burke could articulate words, he knew right away Burke was right for the part.

It was months until Burke was invited to fly to California to audition in person. When the television executives finally offered him the part, he let out a whoop and danced down the hall. After filming at Key West and Los Angeles, Burke went back to his job as a teacher's aide and elevator operator for the New York City Board of Education.

ABC played "Desperate," but decided not to run it as a series. But Burke was more determined than ever to get into acting. He took the pilot tape to an agent and worked hard to create more opportunities for himself.

His performance in "Desperate" was so good that ABC executives wrote a script especially for him. It was a pilot for a series in which he would play a teenager with Down syndrome, the middle child in a working class family. In it, he would struggle to succeed in a public school he attends with his bright younger sister. The executives who planned the show felt they were doing something of value. "We were also giving someone like Chris the chance to prove that they can be total human beings . . . they can have lives of meaning and purpose," recalls Chad Hoffman of ABC. The writers of the program show the main character, Corky Thacher, working hard to achieve his goals and being successful.

The program ran for four successful seasons, and gained enough popularity that it went into syndication (independent stations could purchase episodes for broadcast). At the time Burke's autobiography was written, the program was broadcast in thirty-eight countries — from Australia to Zimbabwe — with more to come.

And Burke himself became a celebrity. In 1991 he was honored as one of ten Outstanding Young Americans. He was nominated for a Golden Globe Award for best supporting actor in a television series. And a school in New York was named after him. Now, instead of people shying away from him, he draws a crowd wherever he goes.

Once Burke's success was established, he decided he wanted to do things to help others — especially others with handicaps. "It was time to give something back," Burke's father said. Burke became a spokesperson for many Down syndrome organizations and helped raise money for the schools he attended. President George Bush invited him to come to the White House to tape a public service announcement on providing opportunities to those with Down syndrome, and introduced Burke as his friend.

Currently he works for the National Down Syndrome Society in New York, and has tackled a new role requiring new skills by becoming editor-in-chief of *News 'n' Views*, a magazine written for, by, and about young adults with Down syndrome. He has made Down syndrome familiar to many people, making it possible for the general public to more comfortably interact with those with the condition.

And Burke's upbeat, can-do approach to life continues to open new doors. (One day, as a child, uncomfortable with the negative implication of the "Down" part of the syndrome's name, he noticed a UPS truck; "Look, Dad! That's what I have. Up syndrome!" he said.) He is a much sought-after speaker among business organizations, traveling all over the world to give speeches and tell business people about what any person with a disability can do if given the chance. He has received a salary from McDonald's to serve as the representative of their McJobs program, through which more than nine thousand people with disabilities have been hired to work in their restaurants.

Burke has inspired many. A pregnant

woman learned through amniocentesis — a process of extracting and analyzing genetic material from a fetus — that her baby had Down syndrome. After watching Burke on "Life Goes On," she decided not to abort the baby but to keep it. Others, those who care for children with Down syndrome, have been emboldened to ask for more and better care for them.

Partly as a result of the example Burke has projected through his show and his public service announcements, others with Down syndrome are being given opportunities. Many who in another time would have died an early death after a useless life are now holding down jobs and living independently.

The composer for the show, Craig Safan, who also has a child with Down syndrome, sees Burke as a hero. "A hero is someone heroic, someone who goes beyond what most people can attain," he says. And considering how little Burke was expected to attain at all, the breadth and value of his accomplishments become particularly meaningful indeed.

WORDS FROM CHRIS BURKE

"The true meaning of life is thinking of others, taking care of yourself, and being happy."

"I care. I'm going to help."

"I like making money but I don't really want to be rich. Just having a job and doing my job and taking care of my family, that's all that counts."

"I've learned from my family to never take my eyes off the goal. I hate the word 'can't'."

Jimmy Carter

Americans who watched television news reports during the last days of the Carter administration usually didn't like what they saw. Some days the coverage featured angry Iranian mobs chanting "Death to America," on others the Ayatollah Khomeini denouncing the United States. President Jimmy Carter tried diplomacy and got nowhere, making him seem even more ineffectual. News anchors tallied how many days the American hostages had been held in Iran, and played and replayed footage of the botched military rescue he'd attempted. With every day that passed, America seemed weaker, more helpless.

The taking of American hostages in Iran wasn't the only episode that eroded the public's faith in Jimmy Carter. Runaway inflation and rising interest rates took their toll as well. And there was also the Soviet invasion of Afghanistan, after which Carter confessed he had learned more about the Soviet Union from that event than he had during his whole term in office. And even though he had been a Democratic president with a Democratic majority in Congress, he lacked the support he needed to carry out his agenda.

And so it was that the man who himself used the word "malaise" to describe the country's mood during his own term in office, was driven in 1980 from that office by a frustrated public. He had become one of the most unpopular presidents in this century; his name became a byword for failed policies.

As a going-away present, his White House staff bought him some stationary power tools for his workshop in Plains, Georgia. And although Carter initially went back to his peanut farm, he wasn't quite ready for a stationary role as home handyman. Writing his memoirs, playing golf, and cashing in on the connections he had made as president was not what Jimmy Carter had in mind. Instead, using his singular diplomatic skills, he has reemerged on the world stage as the most sought-after peacemaker of our time — he even volunteered to help bring an end to the nation's professional baseball players' strike in 1955.

"It's an active intrusion into troubled waters to bring a better life to people," he says of his efforts. "It's not just negotiating an end to a war. It's not just supervising an international election to bring about democracy to

Haiti or the Dominican Republic or to Panama or to Nicaragua, but it's helping to alleviate suffering."

In December of 1994, Carter was on the landing field at Sarajevo, Yugoslavia, putting on a bulletproof jacket and heading into that tumultuous country to try to broker some kind of peace. In September of that year, with American war planes airborne for Haiti, Carter was working with General Colin Powell and Senator Sam Nunn to convince that country's dictator, Raoul Cedras, that it was more courageous to step down from power and avoid conflict than to cause death and destruction.

Earlier still, Carter had worked out a deal with North Korea's Kim Il Sung to end that country's nuclear weapons program. By doing so, he halted a confrontation that had the Clinton administration openly threatening military action.

In 1990, when the Sandinistas were defeated in an election in Nicaragua, Carter was able to appeal directly to the loser, Daniel Ortega, and convince him not to overthrow the elected president, Violeta Chamorro.

And Carter accomplished all this without losing a single American life. Not surprisingly, he is more popular as a former president than he was as a president. In fact, his post-term work has made him the most popular of living past presidents. One young Marine in Haiti said, "You see Carter, give him a kiss for me." It's an ironic twist of fate that he has become so popular simply by continuing to do what he has done all his life: work for what he believes is right.

But not everyone is so happy about the success of his involvements. He gets a surprising amount of criticism from the Washington, D.C. establishment. Every time Carter tries to forge an agreement, he is stepping on the toes of those whose jobs it is to have done so. The ignorant raise questions about who is making America's foreign policy. And foreign governments sometimes object to his involvement as well, fearing that he might be manipulated by other negotiators who simply want there to be more proposals on the table so the parties to an agreement can be played off against each other.

Critics say Carter wants to rehabilitate his image and his place in history after a failed presidency. Others say he simply wants the Nobel Peace Prize. To them, Carter says: "I'd be delighted, not to mention surprised, if just once before I die nobody would suggest that what I'm really trying to do with these years — my hidden agenda — is to win the Nobel Peace Prize."

It's not that Carter would refuse the prize,

70

but his goal is peace, not recognition. "I do what I do because I think it is the right thing to do." Besides, he has wondered, what if his motivation were simply recognition and it never came? "Well, what sort of dried-up, shriveled-up, disappointed, frustrated old prune of a man would I be then? 'Poor ol' Jimmy Carter. He never got his prize.' "

Carter goes about doing whatever he thinks is the right thing to do with a carefully developed style. When negotiating, he first suspends all judgments about the people across the table from him, stripping away whatever prior knowledge he has about them. "That's the critical element of conflict resolution," Carter believes. "The willingness to resist recriminations . . . and the patience to allow them enough time to understand that there's nothing on the table except a mutual effort to reach some sort of agreement.

"Of course, there has to be a table. People in conflict have to be willing to talk about ending it, or at least changing it, and there has to be someone willing to talk to them, however odious they are — and that's where I come in."

When he arrived in Sarajevo, surrounded by blue-helmeted French soldiers and a swarm of reporters, he modestly said, "I have a limited role here." But he was actually there at the invitation of Bosnian Serb leaders, who had sent a delegation more than six thousand miles to Carter's Georgia home to ask him to come and broker a settlement. Although some Clinton administration officials were angry that Carter was even considering going, Carter received permission directly from President Clinton.

"My view," Carter explains, "was that there wasn't much of a peace process anyway. We only get involved in these things when there's no duplication of effort, or when nothing else is working. . . . I decided it was worth at least some effort on my part."

The Clinton administration kept plenty of distance from Carter's effort in order to give him room to maneuver. Clinton asked only that Carter talk to everyone involved in the war — not just the Serbs — a request with which he was easily able to comply, as he never enters a conflict unless he has been assured that he can speak to all sides. Nor does he approach a conflict expecting there to be a winner and loser; each party must ultimately feel a sense of victory.

Now that he is a private citizen, Jimmy Carter has neither elections nor popularity polls to worry about, policy to uphold, or diplomatic protocol or partisanship to defend. He has no power at all except for the office he once held — no authority to broker deals except that which the parties give him. And, he can walk away from — or threaten to walk away from — any discussion he feels is unproductive, which is precisely how he achieved an accord in Bosnia.

When he began negotiations with the Bosnian Serbs, their leader, Radovan Karadzic, told him he would agree to a cease-fire only after international sanctions were lifted. Carter told him that "if that was going to be his position, I'd have to leave immediately and announce that I'd failed." Karadzic realized that Carter would also tell the world why negotiations went nowhere, and the Serb's position would be seen as a fraud. More fruitful discussion ensued.

Carter learned many lessons before becoming such an effective peacemaker. He had been governor of Georgia before he became president, and he was unpopular with the legislature and the public there when he left office. When Carter began his presidency, one of his aides said, "I'm afraid Jimmy will treat Congress like it's the Georgia legislature and Congress will treat him like he's Georgia's governor."

Which is much the way it happened. In those post-Watergate years, Carter enjoyed a Democratic majority in the House and the Senate, yet too often he could not achieve his legislative goals. It may be because he once said he knew more about the issues than members of Congress and that they wasted his time wanting to talk to him. In hindsight, he saw that this approach was arrogant and a political mistake.

Similarly, in 1989, when he monitored the elections in Panama, he didn't want to talk to strongman Manuel Noriega. Consequently, when Noriega stole the election, Carter had no relationship with him and no open door through which to begin negotiations. The only option became military intervention.

But Carter learns from his mistakes. Now, he says: "I'll talk to anybody who wants to talk about peace." As a result, he has communicated with leaders such as Fidel Castro of Cuba, Ethiopia's deposed Mengistu Mariam, and Somalia's Muhammed Farah Aideed. Carter is effective in negotiations, he says, because "I don't take sides. I'm there to listen." He stays neutral, nods, asks an occasional question, and lets people talk.

Although his patience and sympathy are disarming, he can be persistent when the situation calls for it. Decades ago he kept Israel's Menachem Begin and Egypt's Anwar Sadat at Camp David until they reached an agreement. A breakthrough that eventually led to other agreements in the area, the peace he brokered still works today; there's been an overall reduction in tensions and renewed hope for an end to a seemingly endless conflict.

United Nations General Secretary Boutros Boutros-Ghali, who witnessed what Carter accomplished at Camp David, said: "Diplomacy is a multifaceted art, and President Carter understands every aspect it requires: psychological, historical, religious, cultural, and personal. He achieved success then, in the mountains of Maryland, because above all he conveyed to those he encountered a sense of absolute integrity and conviction."

Jimmy Carter is like the prophet who goes unrecognized in his own hometown, but is honored elsewhere. African countries receive him with a dignity usually reserved for heads of state. In the Japanese city of Konu, near Hiroshima, the new Jimmy Carter Civic Center has a museum dedicated to his presidency, and the government of Japan has allocated one million dollars for the Carter Center in Atlanta, which he and his wife, Rosalynn, founded following his defeat by Ronald Reagan.

The Carter Center is a nonpartisan institution with a twenty-five-million-dollar annual budget that works to promote peace and human rights, foster democracy, and fight poverty, hunger, and disease around the world. The center can already claim credit for achieving ninety-five percent eradication of river blindness, a disease carried by blackflies, in Africa and Latin America. Currently, the center's Global 2000 program is attempting to eradicate the Guinea worm, a parasite that has infected as many as two million people each year in sixteen countries in Africa as well as Pakistan and India. Another center program helped introduce a new strain of high-protein corn in Africa, helping to alleviate protein malnutrition.

Carter also initiated The Atlanta Project, which works to improve partnerships between industry and community groups. In addition, it teaches the value of using community-based approaches to solve urban problems and to improve the lives of inner-city residents — an effort that became the national America Project in early 1995.

Carter has also involved himself with Habitat for Humanity, a charitable organization headquartered at Americus, Georgia, about ten miles from Carter's home. He was reluctant to get involved with Habitat at first, but was persuaded of the value of the project, which builds homes for the poor.

A lot of Habitat volunteers came to the Sunday school class he and Rosalynn teach at a Baptist church in Plains. "They began to tell us about how nice the organization was. At first we didn't believe them, but later we learned that they were telling the truth.

"Then, Millard and Linda Fuller [the founders of Habitat] came to us with a long list of things they wanted us to do, which I was resolved I would not do, which I am now doing."

It took fifteen years for Habitat to build its first ten thousand homes, but the next ten thousand went up in two years. By the turn of the century, the organization hopes to be building twenty thousand homes per year. Habitat projects are accomplished with free labor and donations from churches. The volunteers work along with the future homeowners to restore or build housing in their communities. The volunteers are not paid for their work, and this keeps the cost of the housing within reach of the residents. "Habitat for Humanity doesn't give houses away," Carter says. "The new homeowners have to pay the full price, but we don't charge any interest."

Not only is Carter a keynote speaker for some Habitat fund-raising events, he also volunteers a week of his labor every year, sleeping in tents along with the rest of the volunteers. Carter found in Habitat for Humanity not only a way to help others, but also a way to enjoy his favorite hobby — carpentry. He likes to do the more challenging work, such as making sure the windows are square and level and building the porches.

When he's not building Habitat houses, Carter exercises his carpentry skills by making furniture. "Every time Rosalynn needs something, I build it. I like to build things that are actually needed," he says. Cradles are a particular favorite — the one he built for his son Chip has been loaned around the community so often, "some people have had babies they weren't planning to have just so they could use my cradle," Carter once quipped.

Making things with his hands balances his more cerebral pursuits as the world's peace-keeper, as a professor of linguistics at Emory University, and as a writer. "You can only spend five or six hours a day on a word processor, then your mind wants to do something different. So I get out and make a cabinet or a bed or a table or chairs."

He has written eight books since he left office, one of which is a book of poetry, *Always a Reckoning*, published in late 1994. The forty-four poems in the collection — he sent them to and visited Arkansas poet Miller Williams for critique — range in topic from possum hunting to family relationships. He is now among a select group of president/poets, which includes only Abraham Lincoln and John Quincy Adams.

Working as an outsider to politics but an

insider to a foundation has its advantages, Carter notes. "We not only reduce the likelihood of civil wars, domestic wars, direct and indirect human rights oppression, but we also get to know people and their families and their villages in a way that I would never have been able to while I was an incumbent president."

The basic belief that ties together all of Jimmy Carter's efforts is that he has only one life, and therefore only one chance to make it count for something, which Carter sums up as his faith. It's a faith that goes beyond religion or theology; it requires work and effort. "My faith demands — this is not optional — my faith demands that I do whatever I can, wherever I can, whenever I can, for as long as I can, with whatever I have, to try to make a difference."

JIMMY CARTER'S WORDS

"People have a right to their opinions, so basically, I just go about my business."

"I've won elections and I've lost elections and I can assure you that losing is not the end of the world."

"There are people just as good as we are, but not as lucky."

Johnny Cash

Standing onstage at the Grand Old Opry, Johnny Cash was frustrated. The band had just swung into the music for his first song, and the microphone wouldn't budge from its holder. He lost control, consumed by a wave of rage. Johnny Cash yanked the entire stand from the stage and dragged it along the edge, smashing scores of footlights as he struggled with it.

The band stopped playing and the audience sat in shocked silence. Cash was heedless of the shattered glass that was spraying into the front rows. And he was oblivious to the disintegration of his long-standing relationship with the capital of country and western music. He stomped off the stage only to come face-to-face with the manager of the Grand Old Opry.

"We can't use you on the Opry anymore, John," the manager told him. There was nothing for Cash to say — nothing for him to do except stalk out the back door, clamber into his car, and roar off into the night. Out of control from anger and drugs, he smashed into a tree.

This accident caused him a broken nose and jaw. Seven years of drug addiction, cigarettes, and alcohol, though, had already emaciated him — although he's six-foot two, his weight was down to 165 pounds — and reduced his once-deep baritone voice to a hoarse whisper. The car, of course, was a total loss as had been every other car he'd owned in the past seven years. He'd destroyed two Jeeps and a camper, turned over two tractors and a bulldozer, sank two boats in separate accidents on a lake, and jumped from a truck just before it went over a six-hundred-foot cliff.

Fame, even to the extent that Johnny Cash has achieved it, is not synonymous with heroism. Nor is succumbing to drug addiction a heroic act. Nonetheless, Johnny Cash is a hero. Relying on his spiritual life and his friends, he was able to overcome his addictions, rebuild his career and relationships, and go on to serve as an example for others.

As a child (he was born in 1932), listening by lantern light to far-away country music stations on a battery-powered radio in his family's three-room, Arkansas country home, Cash knew he wanted to be a performer. But he didn't realize he would become a pioneer in popular music. Although he'd played jam sessions with Elvis Presley and Jerry Lee Lewis, his career was launched when he appeared as a guest on Presley's show in Memphis in 1955. Soon thereafter, he signed up with Sun Records, the label on which Elvis became famous.

In 1954, after being honorably discharged from the U.S. Air Force, Cash married Vivian Liberto, with whom he had four daughters: Rosanne, Cindy, Tara, and Kathy. But as his career took off, long absences to go on tour put a strain on the marriage. And it was during one of those trips, on a long drive between Miami and Jacksonville in 1957, that Cash was introduced to "bennies," slang for Benzedrine, an amphetamine.

One of the drivers of the two cars making the passage that night pulled over about halfway to Jacksonville and asked if anyone else was sleepy.

"Take one of these. It'll keep you awake," he said. Cash was curious. "Will they hurt you?" he asked.

"They've never hurt me," the driver said. Cash took the pill, and within thirty minutes felt wide awake, refreshed, and talkative. When he got to Jacksonville, he took another pill and felt great for the performance — even though he hadn't slept. Whatever these "bennies" were, Cash made up his mind they were a good thing.

Over the next couple of years, Cash discovered that these pills extended his stamina and performing ability, as well as reduced his preconcert jitters. They made him more talkative, outgoing, a better performer. They did him so much good, he believed, at first, that they were sent by God.

He was soon completely addicted. At the time, few physicians were aware of the dangers of "uppers," and getting prescriptions was an easy matter. By 1960, Cash had developed a standard line; he simply told doctors how he was going to be on the road and needed them in order to be able to meet his commitments. By 1967, however, their side effects had convinced him they were from the devil.

The pills left Cash confused. He found himself unable to think of answers to questions during interviews. Or he would be answering a question and in the middle of it, forget what the question was. He developed a twitch in his neck and face. His eyes were dilated. He fidgeted constantly. And he had near-constant back pain. He was so restless that he walked the floors in the middle of the night, trying to wear off the effects. Or, he would get in the car and go for long, reckless drives.

To come down from his highs, he often took

"downers," or barbiturates, although the drugged unconsciousness he gained could hardly be called rest. Then he would take handfuls of amphetamines to get going again. He often took twenty amphetamines in a day and as many barbiturates to come down.

By the time he moved his family to Los Angeles in 1959, Cash was also drinking heavily. Mixing alcohol with amphetamines often led him to depression. Adding cigarettes to the mix ruined his voice, giving him laryngitis that often lasted for weeks.

Opportunity after opportunity turned into disaster. His performance at Carnegie Hall in New York was a disappointment for his fans because he couldn't speak above a whisper. His appearance on the "Mike Wallace Show" to promote the performance turned into a sullen confrontation during which he made a veiled threat to hit Wallace.

"The longer I took pills, the more unpredictable and violent I got," Cash wrote in his autobiography, *Man in Black*. He found that his friends began to avoid him. "With the continued use of the drug, I lost sight of my obligation to my audience," he recalls. The drug habit also robbed him of his will to be a husband and father, and "voided my conscience, which could no longer govern my judgment."

His marriage ended in 1965, after which he left California and bought himself his dream house near Hendersonville, Tennessee. It was two hundred feet long with a great view of a lake — a real showpiece. Cash invited his family there to observe the anniversary of his brother Jack's death. But Cash's judgment was so twisted from the years of drug abuse that he was totally unprepared for their visit — there was no food in the house, not even enough furniture. June Carter, a performer he had known since his early days in show business, bailed him out by preparing an impromptu dinner, and his family forgave him. Years later he realized how long-suffering they had been during his years of addiction.

He found himself lying to his friends, even breaking the law to smuggle pills into the country. While in El Paso, Texas, he took a trip into Mexico to buy bags full of amphetamines, hiding them in his guitar and his suitcase. Back in El Paso, he was removed from the airplane and arrested. (He was taken into custody seven times during the years he was addicted — usually for public drunkenness.) He traveled handcuffed from the jail to the courthouse, an image captured by news photographers and plastered everywhere, including on the front page of his hometown newspaper in Memphis.

But that was the beginning of the end for drugs in Cash's life. In 1967, in jail again in Lafayette, Georgia, Sheriff Ralph Jones woke up a sick and sober Cash at eight o'clock in the morning. A big fan — he owned every album Cash had made — Jones told Cash it made him heartsick to see the singer wind up in jail again.

Then, Sheriff Jones put Cash's pills on the desk and told him to take them and go. "Now, you can throw the pills away or you can take them and go ahead and kill yourself," Jones told him. "That's exactly what those pills are doing to you. God gave you a free will to do with yourself whatever you want to do."

Cash somberly walked away and threw the pills into the dirt. He told Richard McGibony, the friend who was waiting to pick him up, that he was through with drugs because of what the sheriff had said to him. "God sent him to me, or sent me to him. He made me know. He made me realize I really was about to kill myself. He also made me remember that I really can live."

At first, Cash relapsed into drug abuse, much to his own disappointment and that of those close to him. But eventually he got on track. "I expect to make some wrong decisions in my personal and professional life, as I have many times before," he says, "but I expect to do better as I grow."

Helping him along as he struggled to give up drugs was June Carter. Cash proposed to her in the middle of a performance before five thousand people, and they married in 1968. In 1970, June gave birth to their only son, John Carter Cash. They have performed together for troops in Vietnam, and produced a movie, *Gospel Road*, which Cash has shown to hundreds of thousands of prisoners; Billy and Ruth Graham came to a private screening at the Cash home.

Once he was off drugs, Cash felt it was his obligation to make amends with everyone he had offended or hurt through his addiction. He apologized to people and gave free concerts to make up for the ones he had ruined. Most forgave him readily, but not everyone. Jimmy Dean scolded him for giving all performers a bad reputation, and told Cash how much his behavior had hurt others; they talked a long time, and after Johnny's sincere apology, Dean left smiling.

"How much suffering I would have saved myself and others over the years if I had rebuked and rejected Deception, Pride, Arrogance, and all the other demons . . . and walked always with the Master," Cash reflects. And yet, he also knows he has "been put through the fire" for a reason.

His own failures are what have given him compassion for other, struggling people. "All men are human; all men sin; all men will fall short of your expectations at one time or another," he observes. "Once a Christian puts himself above the world, or in his fervor becomes 'holier than thou' or too good to associate with people of questionable character, then he has alienated the very people who need what he has to share. . . ."

Becoming too good to associate with a group of people of questionable character — prison inmates — is not likely for Cash. He felt a connection to them long before he served any time himself. "I always felt [performing in a prison] was one way of giving back to the American people some of the good they had given us," he says. He performed his first prison concert at Huntsville, Texas State Prison in 1957, just around the time he became involved with drugs, and appeared at San Quentin in 1958 (singer Merle Haggard was an inmate).

The greatest irony is that through his efforts to give back to society, Cash himself reached his greatest heights: the album he recorded in 1968 at California's Folsom Prison was the high-water mark of his career. At his first performance there in 1966, Cash was impressed with the energy the audience brought to the performance. The prisoners had few permitted ways to let off steam, but they were allowed to clap, yell, whistle, stomp their feet, and bang the tables during the show. Cash sensed a rawness and animal power he had felt nowhere else. He wanted to capture that energy in an album.

Cash came to the microphone in the crowded dining room, introduced himself, then sang his "Folsom Prison Blues." There with Cash were his father and June Carter. The album was hugely successful — it sold more than six million copies.

But more important, it inspired people the rest of society had written off. "By doing a prison concert," wrote Cash, "we were letting inmates know that somewhere out there in the free world was somebody who cared for them as human beings. With fewer crimes in our land, on our streets, as our aim, maybe when those men were paroled back into society's mainstream, there'd be less hostility knowing someone had cared."

After the recording, Cash received a letter from one of the inmates: "Dear Johnny, I know now what Jesus meant when he said He was sent to the captives, because I saw Him in you today."

The prisoners were not the only ones touched by Cash: Carl Perkins, a friend and fellow musician who had become an alcoholic, was as well. Perkins was riding in a bus with Cash and June Carter, heading up the coast from San Diego with a hangover from a big drunk, convinced he was dying. Carter reminded him that Cash had overcome his own addiction by turning his problem over to God. Determined to rid himself of liquor, Perkins made up his mind to throw his bottle away.

"Come on, I'll help you," Cash offered.

"No, I'm going to do it myself. If you can do it, so can I," Perkins said. "He's my God, too."

Consequently, Cash's music has become a ministry. "The entertainment world is the front line for spiritual battles," Cash believes. And, since entertainers are seen as leaders and trend setters, Cash views his position as a great responsibility: "I (am) working toward what I was put in this world to do: entertain people; be something worthwhile to them; be an example; be a good influence; stand strong; don't compromise.

"There comes a time in every man's life when he realizes the need to try to accomplish one thing that will say to the world, 'This is the best I had to offer. This is me. This is what I'd like my life to say'," Cash believes. "I know that I must try to let a good light shine and try to live my daily life with charity and tolerance for those whose lives I touch, whether saint or sinner."

In the years since Johnny Cash cleaned up his act, his career has enjoyed a tremendous rebound. He was inducted into both the Country Music Hall of Fame — the greatest honor of his career — and the Rock and Roll Hall of Fame. An album he produced, "American Recordings," features Cash soloing with his guitar. It took longer and cost more to produce than any other record he ever made, but it was the album he had always wanted to do — but couldn't until he'd sobered up.

Cash's sobriety has not been without its temptations. For example, after jaw surgery, he preferred to recover without painkillers, rather than subject himself to the risk. He approaches enticement philosophically: "When you stand with Him, you must renew the stand daily; you must daily be on guard, the hounds of hell are not going to stop snapping at your heels. The devil and his demons aren't going to give up on you as long as they can find a vulnerable spot once in a while," he wrote in his autobiography.

And he now enjoys the rewards of self-control. "I don't smoke, I don't take drugs, I'm in great health, and I feel like I'm singing as good as I was in the fifties," he reflects. "I decided that if I did my best, followed my conscience, took care of my home and family, and prayed daily for wisdom to know what to do, then I need not worry. He'd show me."

JOHNNY CASH'S PHILOSOPHIES

"The more mountains I am climbing, the more I enjoy the view from the top."

"Daddy taught us many things, but a most important lesson was that hard work is good for you."

". . . I'm going to be true not only to those who believe in me and depend on me, but to myself and to God."

"It all comes down to charity. It's the same old lesson: you gain by giving."

"Beware that you brag about standing, lest you fall."

"I must pity those who say they don't believe in God. Even the devil believes in God."

"I hope that if I'm ever arrested for being a Christian, there'll be enough evidence to convict."

Bill Cosby

Bill Cosby's sixth-grade teacher was fed up. Here was a boy who was very bright — in fact intelligence tests later identified him as a gifted student — a boy smart enough to learn or do just about anything he wanted. But all the Cosby boy seemed to want to do was clown for his friends.

Rather than do his homework, Cosby was out on the sidewalks of North Philadelphia, the narrow brick row houses packed side by side, the vacant lots sparkling with broken glass. It was a dead-end life for a black boy in the big city — a life of underachievement beckoned.

"I was really afraid to do these things, because it meant work," Cosby has said. He avoided the work so much he flunked the tenth grade. And, instead of going back and repeating the grade, Cosby dropped out of high school. That's when he learned the hard realities of life. The boy who avoided school-work found himself shining shoes and delivering groceries to help support the family.

To get away, Cosby joined the U.S. Navy in 1956, but after only three weeks of serving under people less intelligent than himself, he decided he was better off going to college. "I changed from an underachiever to a point where I realized that I had to get out and earn it," Cosby remembers.

Cosby learned that hard work is the answer to many problems, and he ultimately became one of the most financially successful entertainers of all time. But he has also achieved something far more meaningful. He has addressed one of America's gravest problems — strengthening and promoting the family — with a convincing, nearly contagious optimistic humor.

Bill Cosby spent his four years in the navy wisely. He earned a high-school equivalency diploma through correspondence courses, and also learned to be a physical therapist. Once out of the navy, he returned to Philadelphia and attended Temple University with the help of a track and field scholarship. He was tempted to become a professional athlete, perhaps even playing for the Green Bay Packers football team, but as a sophomore he found his calling: telling jokes at a local coffeehouse. Soon Cosby was performing at New York coffeehouses such as Greenwich Village's Gaslight Cafe, where Woody Allen and other comedians have gotten their start, yet again quitting school.

"My mind was not on books [at Temple] but on bookings; and so, I dropped out to go into show business, a career move as sound as seeking my future as a designer of dirigibles," Cosby admits. "Although my mother and father kept telling me that I should finish college before I flopped in show business, I felt that only *I*, with the full wisdom of a North Philadelphia jock, knew what was best for me.

"I believed it was my destiny to make people laugh. These people, of course, did not include my mother and father, who felt that if there had been any value in stand-up comedy, Temple would have offered it for three credits."

In a manner of speaking, Cosby's personal involvement with fatherhood can be said to be the result of a blind date with Camille Hanks, who in the early 1960s was a psychology student at Stedman College in Atlanta. They married in 1964 and have raised five children.

Shortly after the wedding, Cosby made television history when he starred opposite Robert Culp in the "I Spy" series. "I Spy" was the first program that paired a black actor as an equal with a white co-star — a role that earned him three Emmy Awards.

He also won the respect and appreciation of Coretta Scott King, widow of slain civil rights leader Dr. Martin Luther King, Jr. "I didn't fully appreciate his extraordinary personal decency until my husband was assassinated in 1968 and Bill and his "I Spy" co-star, Robert Culp, came to my home to pay their respects," King recalled. "Many of those who visited during those difficult days offered their help, but it was the "I Spy" team who provided the support that I needed most, comforting my children while I met with an endless stream of visitors who came to express their condolences. Throughout the day, Cosby and Culp were there, playing and talking with the kids, even getting the youngsters to laugh a little."

Cosby continues to use humor to address problems, and one of the issues he feels most strongly about is that families are extremely important. "Just what is a father's role today?," he asks. "As a taskmaster he's inept. As a referee, he's hopeless. And as a short-order cook, he may have the wrong menu. The answer, of course, is that no matter how hopeless or copeless a father may be, his role is simply to *be* there. . . ."

In an age when more than half the children in this country will spend at least part of their youth without a father in the home, Bill Cosby stands like a lighthouse in a treacherous sea. In his highly successful "The Cosby Show" and in his book, *Fatherhood*, Cosby hammers home the message to fathers: "Be there with your children. Be there."

In "The Cosby Show," which ran from 1984 to 1992, Cosby created a niche for himself — America's number-one father figure, Dr. Cliff Huxtable. As Huxtable, Cosby showed parents how to truly listen to children and to respect them while not giving up their own authority. He taught the world about the value of strong, caring parents and the importance of honesty and openness in family communications. At a time when family comedy was taking a backseat to sex and violence, "The Cosby Show" became the first television sitcom to present serious child-rearing and parenting issues. Wrote one television critic: "Cosby was a great salesman for the family. He made family life look like so much fun, I decided to have one."

One reason the show was so influential is that it did not present itself as a program strictly for a black audience. Rather, it is a program that happens to feature a black cast, transcending race. "In traveling around the country, hearing a lot of anecdotal material, a lot of whites have used Cosby as a model for being a father," says Alvin F. Poussaint, M.D., a professor at Harvard University who consulted on each episode of the show. "Cosby was also able to help them use humor and see their family in a different way as a result of the show." Without knowing it, viewers were being challenged to reevaluate their family roles while they were educated in parenting skills.

Yet however much Cosby enjoys being funny, there are also times when he opts for seriousness. "The male has got to get rid of the feeling that inflating his wife makes him a man, that mere fertilization is a reason for a high five," Cosby wrote in *Fatherhood*. In fact, Cosby's book scolds those who hold to that viewpoint: "Some males, unfortunately, are interested only in impregnating a woman to become a biological father and have no interest in becoming a psychological father: a man who helps to raise and support his children. Fathers who willingly abandon their offspring are shortsighted and irresponsible. They shortchange their children, their families, society, and themselves."

Cosby is calling on fathers in particular to care for, nurture, and discipline their children in a spirit of love and humor. Studies have shown that children with fathers in the home tend to get along better with their peers and display more social confidence. They face new situations better and score higher on intelligence and aptitude tests. They are typically more responsible.

And the most reliable predictor of a child's academic performance is family background. Some children who grow up without fathers develop conduct disorder, or uncontrolled rage at adults, at society, and at life in general. The anger may smolder for years and then, at the slightest provocation, erupt in violence.

With the rise of the single-parent family, many men feel marginal, even superfluous in raising children. To them, Cosby offers words of encouragement: "If the new American father feels bewildered and even defeated, let him take comfort from the fact that whatever he does in any fathering situation has a fifty percent chance of being right. . . . There are no absolutes in raising children." The only people who are always sure about the right way to raise children, Cosby contends, are those who have never had any.

Cosby, then, as a father of five, can't always be sure about raising children, although he can certainly speak with authority. (Each of the Cosby children was given a name beginning with "E" — Erika, Erinn, Ennis, Ensa, and Evin. The "E," Cosby explains, is for "excellence," something he insisted his children strive for in their schoolwork.)

With parenthood Cosby began to see things from his own parents' perspective. Like himself, some of his five children doubted the value of education. His son Ennis began receiving bad grades when he was thirteen. The boy told his father he didn't want the pressure of studying — that he wanted to be "regular people." The encounter became the germ for an idea played out within the Huxtable family (many themes worked through on the program originated within Cosby's own family). Theo Huxtable tells his father that good grades don't matter for someone who wants to be a "regular person." Huxtable listens silently, deadpan, then proclaims: "That is *the most* ridiculous thing I have ever heard."

And that is Cosby's view of education: it is absolutely necessary. "At forty-nine, I was trying to tell all these people that they should finish their formal education and then go on to be what they wanted to be. I was beginning to fear, however, that they would never *know* what they wanted to be, even when they got to *be* it."

Earlier on, Cosby had realized that he had to set an educational example. The high-school and college dropout had to redeem himself. He wrote a 242-page dissertation in 1977, and the University of Massachusetts at Amherst awarded him a doctorate of education degree. The dissertation drew on his work in children's television, including "Fat Albert and the Cosby Kids," his appearances on "Sesame Street" and "The Electric Company," and his teaching experience in prisons.

During Cosby's career, his twenty-four comedy albums have sold more copies than any others. He has starred in movies such as *Mother, Jugs and Speed, Mickey and Boggs* and *Uptown Saturday Night*, and is in big demand in nightclubs. He's a successful author as well. Two of his books, *Fatherhood* and *Time Flies* have been number-one best-sellers, in part because they address serious issues in a light-hearted way. *Time Flies* deals with aging, and Cosby wrote it to observe his passage to age fifty. He deals with the consequent problems with typical humor: "People with sometime memories like mine should tell only the shortest possible stories."

Cosby's intent has never been to build himself up as the ideal father. He'd prefer to boost the status of fathers and mothers as a group. To young people looking for role models, he says: "Forget about the celebrities. We're not gods; we're not perfect and we have our problems. . . . The image is sitting right there in your home." It is their own parents Cosby urges children to consider as examples. "Have you ever bothered to look at your mother who cooks breakfast, gets on the bus, rides to clean somebody's house, comes back, makes your dinner, and gives you money for some records or a stereo? . . . Tell me that is not a positive image. Tell me that your father who comes home and changes clothes to go to his second job to support you by working eighteen hours a day is not a positive image."

Positive images are what Cosby has been diligently creating throughout his professional life. For too long television has portrayed blacks in demeaning, undignified, and stereotypical roles, he maintains. He says television producers have an image of blacks as "the funny minstrel. They think of us as living cartoons." He calls it the "drive-by mentality," because those who keep blacks in the old molds "drive by a black housing project and take a quick look. They see the pimp, the dealer, the strutting kids. What they never see, because they don't want to look for it, is the hardworking mother and father upstairs who are trying to move up and out. You see, there's nothing *funny* in that."

The solution, Cosby maintains, is that "someone at the very top has to say 'Okay, enough of this'." That person has been Bill Cosby himself. By being a successful person in his work and in his family, he is showing others not only that it can be done, but how to do it, providing an especially important example to those struggling with the crushing weight of problems caused by the crises in families, weight borne disproportionately by African-Americans.

To this reality, Bill Cosby focuses on what has to be the solution for each individual regardless of race: strong families raise strong, healthy children. He also knows that black children must receive positive messages about themselves. This is why he brushed aside critics of "The Cosby Show" who said the program was unrealistic. Cosby played a physician, and his co-star, Phyllicia Rashad, played an attorney. "I was aiming to break a mold," Cosby explained. By breaking that mold, he has helped to set people free.

BILL COSBY COMMENTS
(EXCERPTED FROM FATHERHOOD)

"A father's job is *not* to get tired of what he has a right to get tired of. . . . A father has to keep hanging around and loving and knowing that his baby needs guidance because her own rudder hasn't started working yet. Keep trying and keep having patience. *That* is fatherhood."

"Raising children is an incredibly hard and risky business in which no cumulative wisdom is gained: each generation repeats the mistakes the previous one made."

"No matter how much money you have, you will never be able to buy your kids everything they want. The great American trap is trying to make a child happy by buying something. . . ."

"Cosby's First Law of Intergenerational Perversity: No matter what you tell your child to do, he will always do the opposite. . . . Even though your kids will consistently do the exact opposite of what you tell them to do, you have to keep loving them just as much."

"Nothing is harder for a parent than getting your kids to do the right thing. . . . Although we try hard to inspire our kids to do good work on their own, the motivation for such work always has to come from inside them; and if the kids really don't want to study, don't want to achieve, then we must not feel guilty; we are not at fault."

"The only reason we had children was

to give them love and wisdom and then freedom. But it's a package deal: the first two have to lead to the third."

Elizabeth Dole

No sooner had Hurricane Andrew finished blasting its way through Florida in 1992 than Elizabeth Dole, president of the American Red Cross (ARC), was landing at the Miami airport to get a firsthand assessment of the devastation.

It was late at night when she drove past downed power lines, overturned cars, and neighborhoods that had been literally wiped off the map. She became thoroughly lost as she tried to navigate the pitch-black maze of streets, their signs blown away with the wind.

Police were on duty, alert to curfew violators and possible looters. When an officer spotted her car maneuvering through the chaos, he pulled her over. She told him who she was and what her mission was and, grateful for her presence, he shared his soda pop and cookies with her.

Many people were lost in Florida that night — their homes destroyed or damaged. The havoc was unimaginable to Dole, even though after a year at the helm of the American Red Cross she had already seen suffering beyond the imagination of most people. But the reorganization she had accomplished at the Red Cross proved its value that night.

Disaster operations kicked into high gear. An army of twelve thousand volunteers was at work, and they housed eighty-five thousand people in 230 shelters, served nearly five million meals, and provided sixty thousand families with vouchers so they could replace food, clothing, medicine, and other essentials lost in the storm.

Although it was a major effort, the Hurricane Andrew relief was just one part of the Red Cross's duties in the United States. With thirty thousand paid staff and one and a half million volunteers, the organization is responsible for collecting, testing, and distributing more than half of America's blood supply, teaching life-saving health and safety classes to eleven million people per year, and providing food, shelter, and hope to those whose lives are turned upside down by the forces of nature. The International Red Cross, of which the ARC is a member, provides humanitarian and relief services to victims of natural and man-made disasters, as well as helping refugees fleeing zones of conflict.

Mention the name Dole in Washington,

D.C., and some people first think of Senate majority leader, Robert Dole of Kansas, the ranking Republican in Washington and a promising candidate for president. But others are just as apt to think of Elizabeth Dole, his equally influential wife.

She was born Mary Elizabeth Alexander Hanford in historic Salisbury, North Carolina, on July 29, 1936. She lived an upper-middle-class life in a Methodist family. The Hanfords lived in an English-style brick-and-stucco house with a spiral staircase; magnolia trees graced the front yard. Her interest in politics first surfaced when she was elected president of her third-grade bird club.

She attended Duke University in Durham, North Carolina, where she was elected student government president, was crowned May Queen and was chosen for membership in the Phi Beta Kappa honorary society. She went abroad in 1959 to study English history and government at Oxford University. Next she got a job at the Harvard Law School library, and worked for North Carolina Senator B. Everett Jordan on Capitol Hill.

In 1962, she was one of two dozen women to enroll in Harvard Law School. On her first day at Harvard, a male student asked her why she was there. "Don't you realize that there are men who would give their right arm to be in this law school — men who would use their legal education?," he said. One law professor refused to acknowledge his female students except for the one day a year when he required them to read an original poem before the rest of the class. But she refused to let such experiences stand in her way; she was elected president of the International Law Club and, before she graduated in 1965, she was also elected class secretary, a life-time position.

After law school she applied for one of fifteen White House Fellowships, positions in which young professionals spend a year working with cabinet-level presidential appointees. There were three thousand applicants, and although she was one of eighteen finalists, she was not selected. "You learn from your losses," she said of the experience.

After passing the bar exam in 1966, she worked at the Department of Health, Education, and Welfare and took legal cases for indigents. She was almost thirty-two in 1968 when she was hired as a representative of the federal government's efforts in consumer affairs, working out of the White House.

Dole's work with the Red Cross is her most recent undertaking in a long career of public service. She was deputy director of the White House Office of Consumer Affairs under President Richard Nixon. It was there that she began a career-long dedication to public safety, for

BOOKS BLOW THE BLUES AWAY

the National Safety Coun-
Service Award in 1989.
1987, when Dole was sec-
tion under President Ronald
y enjoyed its safest maritime,
way records in history. Her
as many lives as possible as
. That meant providing in-
already available automobile
olutely necessary in rear-end
es — and the production of
ent additional protection in
ular crashes. The rules were
a vigorous competition be-
of state safety-belt laws and
ir bags and automatic belts,
oth.
any safety initiatives she
requirements for air bags
y belts in all new cars. She
le for rear-window brake
me standard equipment on
1986.
usade to raise the drinking
; she directed the overhaul
of the aviation safety inspection system; and
she imposed tougher aviation security measures at domestic airports, which in turn led
to tighter security measures around the world.

113

She also oversaw the sale of CONRAIL, the government-owned railroad, which returned two billion dollars to the United States Treasury, a flagship effort in the privatization of American government.

As secretary of labor under President George Bush, beginning in January, 1989, she worked to help shatter the "glass ceiling" for America's working women and minorities. The Department of Labor investigated whether qualified women and minorities were included in developmental programs, rotational assignments, reward structures, and training programs, the indicators of upward mobility in corporate America. When she was secretary of labor, sixty-two percent of her senior staff were women or minorities.

She explains her activism for women's rights this way: "Over the years, women have more and more come to realize that power is a positive force if it is used for positive purposes. We women have come to realize that we cannot have an impact on the issues we care about unless we have a place at the policy table, unless we direct public attention to our cause by aggressive and creative promotion through the media and other outlets and, in some instances, unless we get out and raise the necessary money."

She also worked to increase safety and

health in the workplace and upgrade the skills of the American workforce. She helped improve relations between labor and management, playing, for example, a key role in the resolution of the bitter Pittston Coal Strike.

After twenty-five years of government service, Dole resigned in 1990 to assume leadership of the Red Cross. When Congress is debating a tax bill, it's Bob Dole's face Americans see on the evening news. But when floods hit the Midwest or an earthquake hits California, Elizabeth Dole, the first woman since Clara Barton to serve as Red Cross president, is on the front line, coordinating the disaster relief.

"Serving as president of the American Red Cross has been the most rewarding and fulfilling job of my life," she has said. Through the Red Cross, the world's foremost humanitarian organization, she has been able to organize and energize other people who share her compassionate heart. In 1991, her first year in office, she was herself a member of the volunteer force, declining her $200,000 salary. "The best way I can let volunteers know of their importance is to be one of them," she explained.

During her first month on the job at the Red Cross she traveled to Kuwait just after Iraqi occupation forces were ejected during the Persian Gulf War. She met with General Norman Schwartzkopf to discuss Red Cross service to American service personnel there, and then she went to an institution for physically and mentally handicapped children in Kuwait City.

It was a nightmare. There was no electricity, no running water, and only 22 nurses for 374 patients. While the Iraqis had occupied Kuwait, 170 of the patients had died and many of the medical staff had fled the country. The walls were pocked with bullet holes from gunfire directly over the beds where children lay in the dark.

"No one could see the suffering of these innocent children and not want to do something," Dole said. "On the spot I pledged that the American Red Cross would send fifty nurses, doctors, and physical therapists." Within weeks, nurses and physicians from across America answered the Red Cross call for help, some giving up paid jobs, all leaving friends and families to take on this hardship assignment.

Dole has also visited Africa, where many wars have led to famines and great suffering. After touring Somalia, she said, "Vivid images of that mission will haunt me the rest of my life."

She found a little boy lying under a sack in Baidoa. He was so emaciated she thought he was dead, but the boy's brother sat him up. She asked for some camel's milk to feed him, and as she raised the cup to his mouth, she put her arm around his back. "The feeling of the little bones almost piercing through his flesh is something I will never forget," she said. "That is when the horror of starvation becomes real — when you can touch it."

In Bardera, there was a bloody shirt on the stairs of the Red Cross headquarters. A religious leader had been shot when looters broke into his home the night before, and a Red Cross doctor operated by flashlights for hours. When the patient died, the doctor feared retribution. "And in our little field hospital, I saw four severely malnourished people with gunshot wounds, shot by looters who burst into the Red Cross feeding station to steal food from these desperately poor people."

That was where she met Anika, a Red Cross worker in her twenties, who had just started her six-month assignment. "Red Cross workers — the true unsung heroes and heroines of so many disasters — placing themselves in harm's way to help their fellow man. That memory, also, will remain with me forever," Dole recalled.

When genocidal warfare broke out in the central African country of Rwanda, Elizabeth Dole traveled there, too. "It is very difficult to describe the horror that is Rwanda," she said. "When I arrived at the Rwandan border in Goma, Zaire, it was only the second day of body collection. The bodies still lined the roads, waiting for pick-up."

Humanitarian efforts were more difficult because of conditions on the ground. The water, for example, was contaminated. Latrines and even graves were all but impossible to dig in the lava rock ground. To top it off, Goma is so remote from points of distribution that simply getting supplies there was chaotic. And the refugees were more afraid of returning home than of dying in a strange land.

"As I walked through the camp," Dole recounted, "a child about six years old came up to me and took my hand — so trusting — following me wherever I went. I wonder where this child is now. What kind of future is there for him?"

Fortunately, many of Elizabeth Dole's experiences have happy endings. For example, in Croatia she came across a little girl named Jasmina Ceric who, with her mother and sister, had been separated from her father for months while he was held in a detention camp. The Red Cross was able to learn that Mr. Ceric had been released, and father and daughter were reunited. David Sager, a Connecticut man who saw the televised report of their reunion, brought the family to live in America. Later, they came to visit Dole at ARC headquarters in Washington, D.C.

"Staying ahead of the curve" is a priority at the Red Cross now. While it is impossible to predict where and when the next disasters will occur, they will happen somewhere, sometime. To be prepared, Dole launched a Control Center that allows the Red Cross to monitor current disasters and impending threats, and to direct disaster operations around the clock, seven days per week.

The Red Cross has quadrupled the number of trained disaster-relief experts and positioned millions of dollars worth of communications equipment and disaster resources in strategic locations around the country in order to shorten response time and to improve services to victims. "The part I love is that you deal with dire human needs on a full-time basis," Dole says. "It is really a joy to feel a positive difference in people's lives."

In May of 1991, just five months after her arrival at the Red Cross, Elizabeth Dole announced the most ambitious and far-reaching project the organization has ever undertaken — a $148-million total transformation of Red Cross blood operations. As a billion-dollar enterprise operating in a highly regulated environment, American Red Cross Blood Services collects, tests, and processes more than six million units of blood from more than four million volunteer blood donors every year.

Since World War II, there had been only two tests for infectious disease performed on each unit of donated blood. With the advent of HIV/AIDS and medical advances that make the presence of certain diseases detectable, the Red Cross now performs eight tests on every unit of blood. In fact, it is estimated that one hundred million more tests were conducted in the second five years of the 1980s than were done in the first half of that decade. With each test introducing the need for new protocols and quality assurance procedures, the Red Cross infrastructure built incrementally over the last forty years was becoming overburdened and outmoded.

The ongoing modernization effort includes the creation of the largest blood information data base in the world for transfusion medicine research; the establishment of an unsurpassed quality assurance system; the construction of nine state-of-the-art national testing laboratories, which are the best in the world, to replace more than fifty aging and semi-independent regional labs; the development of a single standardized computer system that links all Red Cross blood operations and replaces twenty-eight different computer systems that had been developed, programmed, and reprogrammed over the years; and the founding of the Charles Drew Biomedical Institute, a technology-based education and training institute that will deliver the latest in techniques and tools to Red Cross personnel. Located in Washington, D.C., the Drew Institute was hailed by Federal Drug Administration Commissioner David Kessler as "exceptionally well suited for seeking and achieving the highest standards not only among ARC blood banks, but throughout the industry. The nation and the FDA," he added, "applaud the American Red Cross and this institute for rising to the challenge."

While Senator Dole has been a candidate for president and vice president, by all outward appearances the balance of power in the Dole's relationship seems relatively equal. A former debutante with the good manners of the sorority house and the political instincts of the back room, Elizabeth Dole attracts fans of both sexes and political persuasions. *Esquire* magazine lauded her as one of the "Women We Love" and a 1988 Gallup poll named her as one of the world's ten most admired women.

In 1993, she received a Lifetime Achievement Award from the Women Executives in State Government for helping women and minorities. She was also inducted into the Safety and Health Hall of Fame International for her many transportation, workplace, and blood safety accomplishments. She also received the North Carolina Press Association's first "North Carolinian of the Year" Award.

The couple met in 1972 when Elizabeth Dole was serving as deputy to Virginia Knauer, a Republican from Pennsylvania who was President Nixon's choice to head the President's Committee on Consumer Interests. She and Knauer visited Senator Dole to discuss a consumer plank in the Republican platform for the presidential election that year. She was thirty-nine when they married in 1975; he was fifty-two. The two discuss their marriage in *Unlimited Partners*, their 1988 autobiography.

Good humor has kept their marriage solid. Once, at a 1984 joint appearance at the Gridiron Dinner, an annual light-hearted media and local dignitary roast, Bob jokingly declared that Dole would not be a candidate for president. Elizabeth jumped to her feet and said: "Speak for yourself, sweetheart."

At the same roast, when the senator was asked if being married to a powerful woman made him feel emasculated, she quipped, "Hold it, cupcake. I'll take this one."

Elizabeth Dole confesses that her job at the ARC entails "moments of incredible sadness. Indeed, I have been asked many times how Red Crossers can continue to work day after day in places like Rwanda and Bosnia without giving up. And it's true that no matter how many people we are able to help, we know there are others who suffer."

Yet she is able to continue caring for others without limits because of her faith. "My faith means a lot to me. I don't feel that I have to do it all on my own. I think I can face challenging situations and feel there's a source of strength beyond myself, that it's not all just on my shoulders. . . .

"What we do on our own matters little — what counts is what God chooses to do through us. Life is more than a few years spent on self indulgence or career advancement. It's a privilege, a responsibility, and a stewardship to be met according to His calling."

ADVICE FROM ELIZABETH DOLE

"Always plan for the unexpected."

"Trust your instincts."

"Maintain your integrity."

"Demonstrate a commitment to those who follow."

"Do not let others define success for you."

Betty Ford

Betty Ford looked out the window of her hospital room and saw the newspeople gathering below. As a matter of fact, their floodlights shined up at her window as if she were some kind of fugitive.

She wasn't, but she didn't want the attention just then, either. She was spending the night in the Presidential Suite at the Naval Medical Center at Bethesda, Maryland, where the window was low enough for the television cameras to get a good shot of her. She was waiting to find out if she had cancer.

She had gone to her doctor for a routine checkup just the day before. But when the physician examined her breast, he frowned and came back with a specialist.

"I still didn't think much about it," she wrote. "Doctors had been checking portions of my anatomy for so long — ever since the pinched nerve, really — that I could take quite a bit of poking and prodding and hearing murmurs of 'Mmmm,' and go right on wondering when I was going to be able to attack the huge pile of mail that was waiting on my desk."

Indeed, if there were a problem, it would be just one more that Ford would shrug off and deal with. For years she had been taking various pills for a pinched nerve, arthritis, and muscle spasms in her neck.

The specialist examined her, and told her they wanted to operate immediately. "Well they can't operate immediately," she snapped. "I have a full day tomorrow." And it occurred to her how strange it is that people try to hang onto the known, the normal, and the routine in the face of upsetting news. Like any other woman under the same circumstances, she clung to her daily schedule — but her activities could hardly be called normal. Her day involved ceremonies, speeches, and luncheons.

After meeting her commitments, she checked into the hospital, and her husband drove back to an empty, lonely White House. Ford had an intuition that the lump was malignant, but those around her continued to hope that it wasn't. The doctors were going to perform a biopsy of the lump; if it was cancer, they would remove her breast.

When Ford awoke in the recovery room, she learned that her doctors had found cancer in three of her lymph nodes as well as in her breast, indicating that it had already begun to spread. The cancerous breast had been removed. Just like that, a big question mark loomed over the Ford family, and the nation. There was no way of knowing how long she would live.

Though breast cancer had previously been a hush-hush subject, as long as the public already knew, thanks to a press release her husband had issued and to relentless media coverage, Ford decided to go ahead and talk about her surgery. "I got a lot of credit for having gone public with my mastectomy, but if I hadn't been the wife of the president of the United States, the press would not have come racing after me," she wrote in her autobiography *The Times of My Life*. "So in a way, it was fate."

And perhaps it was more even than that. "God moves in a mysterious way His wonders to perform," she said. She lay in bed and watched television shows about women lining up to go in for breast examinations because of her. One of them was Happy Rockefeller, wife of Vice President Nelson Rockefeller. Three weeks after the president's wife lost a breast, so did the vice president's. Today the list includes names such as Shirley Temple Black, Nancy Reagan, Ann Jillian, and Olivia Newton-John.

Betty Ford broke open the taboo on talking

about breast cancer. But there is more. Ford also brought alcohol and drug addiction to the forefront of public awareness when she candidly told the world that, after having taken medication after medication for myriad physical ailments, she had a problem with liquor and pills and was going in for treatment. She expressed her bitterness at the medical profession "after fourteen years of being advised to take pills, rather than wait for the pain to hit. I took pills for pain. I took pills to sleep. I took mild tranquilizers. . . . It was easier to give a woman tranquilizers and get rid of her than to sit and listen."

Thanks to Betty Ford's candor, discussing one's chemical dependence has become as destigmatized as talking about breast cancer. Thanks to Betty Ford, going for help has become acceptable. Perhaps more than any other individual, she has launched the movement for women's health care issues.

"I am an ordinary woman who was called on stage at an extraordinary time," she says. "I was no different once I became first lady than I had been before. But through an accident of history, I became interesting to people."

Her early life could not have been much more ordinary. She was born Elizabeth Anne Bloomer in Chicago on April 8, 1918 and was raised in Grand Rapids, Michigan. She was the third child and only daughter of Hortense Neahr and William Stephenson Bloomer. Her father was a traveling salesman for the Royal Rubber Co., and sold conveyor belts to factories. He died from carbon monoxide poisoning in the family garage when she was a teenager. Later, her mother remarried.

Raised with two older brothers, Betty Bloomer was something of a tomboy and used to get into mischief as a kid, especially around Halloween. "Instead of trick or treat, we'd go on a rampage called 'garbage night.'

We tipped over everybody's garbage pails, white-washed everybody's porches, soaped everybody's windows. We did things so terrible I would be furious if my children had ever tried them. . . . We were really nasty kids."

But the phase didn't last long. She became confirmed in the Episcopal Church and developed a passion for dancing. After she graduated from high school in 1936, she attended two sessions of the Bennington School of Dance in Bennington, Vermont. There she met and began a friendship with Martha Graham that would last until the great dancer's death in 1991. After two summer sessions at Bennington, she convinced her mother to allow her to go to New York and continue her studies at the Graham School. Eventually she performed as a member of Graham's troupe.

But Betty Bloomer's mother prevailed on her to come back to Grand Rapids when World War II was about to begin. Instead of pursuing her dream to become a dancer, she became a fashion coordinator at a department store and formed her own dance group, teaching handicapped children.

When she was twenty-four, she married Bill Warren; the wedding took place in her parent's home, although they didn't approve of him. Warren had diabetes and therefore was not bound for service in the war; instead, the newlyweds traveled to various cities as Warren tried to get a career as a furniture salesman going. When they lived in Maumee, Ohio, she commuted to nearby Toledo to work in a department store and to teach dance at Toledo University. The marriage was not a particularly happy one and ended after five years.

Betty Bloomer Warren wasn't single for long. Soon after moving back to Grand Rapids, she became acquainted with Jerry Ford, whose reputation around Grand Rapids was well known. He was a football star, and went on to the University of Michigan. He became a lieutenant in the navy during the war, and by 1947, when she returned to Grand Rapids, he was preparing to run for Congress. They were engaged in 1948, and the wedding took place two weeks before he was elected to his first term in office. She was thirty and he was thirty-five.

"When he met Mom, he was the All-American guy, college football, law school, navy, Yale, good looking, running for Congress, the whole shot," wrote their son Steve in her other autobiography, *Ford: A Glad Awakening*. "Who wouldn't want to be married to him? That's what dreams are made of."

They lived for many years in Alexandria, Virginia, where their children — Mike, Jack, Steve, and Susan — were raised. When the children were young, Ford dedicated her time to the Episcopal Church, the Republican party, Boy Scouts, Girl Scouts, and other family activities. She was a congressional wife, and it took its toll.

"Dad is one of those guys who delegate responsibility," wrote Steve. "Everybody has his responsibility, and you put your head down and get it done. He never starts a project and quits, and he expects other people to be the same way."

That's how problems started. Ford's career in Congress was moving ahead, and his wife felt she was being left behind. She had no college degree, and her husband's advancements increased her sense of inferiority. "He gets all the headlines and praise, but what about me?," she wrote. "The more important Jerry became, the less important I became."

Life didn't get any better in 1973, when Gerald R. Ford was appointed to finish Spiro Agnew's term as vice president. Nor did they improve in August of 1974, when he was sworn in as the thirty-eighth president of the United States. A few weeks later, President Ford pardoned Richard Nixon; eighteen days later came Betty Ford's surgery.

After her mastectomy came an outpouring of feeling for her from all over the country. Newspaper articles and editorials, prayers, cards, and letters — fifty thousand pieces of mail in all. "Lying in the hospital, thinking of all those women going for cancer checkups because of me, I'd come to recognize more clearly the power of the woman in the White House," she explains. "Not *my* power, but the power of the position, a power which could be used to help." She remembered that her mother had admired Eleanor Roosevelt; now, in the same position as that former first lady, she would be a role model to others.

The message of Betty Ford's experience is simple: there is no shame in any problem you have, as long as you go for help. She was willing to talk about her own situation, and the issues of the country, in an open, candid way. "I tried to be honest; I tried not to dodge subjects. I felt the public had a right to know where I stood. Nobody had to feel the way I felt. I wasn't forcing my opinions on anybody, but if someone asked me a question, I gave that person a straight answer."

Americans loved her honesty, coming as it did on the heels of the Watergate scandal. "I believe my reputation for outspokenness is partly due to my coming after Mrs. Nixon, who was very quiet and never thrust herself forward," Ford hypothesizes. "Since for the most part I did what came naturally, I was somewhat astonished to find I'd become one of the most popular women in the world. I loved it. I'd be dishonest if I said it didn't please me. I hadn't expected it, but so long as it was forthcoming, I enjoyed it."

She knew that people identified with her. Formerly divorced, having been to a psychiatrist, having various physical problems, and feeling she was living in her husband's shadow, made it possible for ordinary people to relate to her. "They knew I was no different from them, it was just that fate had put me in this situation."

When Ford was in the White House, she often pressed her husband with issues that were important to her, such as the Equal

Rights Amendment, which would constitutionally protect women's rights. Although it has not come to pass, Ford's support of it made it respectable. She also worked for handicapped children and the arts — urging her husband, despite his reluctance, to award the Presidential Medal of Freedom to Martha Graham. "You know, if you bring up a subject long enough with a man, why, finally he gets so tired of it he agrees to anything," she joked at the time. It was no secret that she had become much more popular than he; the president often jokingly referred to himself as Betty Ford's husband.

The Ford family was out of the White House living in the California desert town of Rancho Mirage, before Betty Ford's problem with alcohol and drugs finally surfaced. Most people close to the chemically dependent never confront the issue because they fear the rage that would be their reward. Nonetheless, Ford's daughter, Susan, who found herself staying away from home because of her mother's condition, tried unsuccessfully to talk to her mother about her problem. Then, instead of waiting for her to come to the end of her rope and call for help, her family and others significant and important to her intervened to help her despite herself.

One day, Ford's entire family filed into the

room she'd been in by herself and closed the door. Then they told her, one at a time, how her drinking and drug usage had hurt them. "Well, they hurt me back. All of them hurt me. I collapsed into tears. But I still had enough sense to realize they hadn't come around just to make me cry; they were there because they loved me and wanted to help me."

Betty Ford soon checked into the Long Beach Naval Hospital for treatment for alcohol and drug dependence. She was put in a room with four beds — her, a former first lady. But part of her problem had been that, as the president's wife, doctors didn't want to anger her, and issued whatever prescription she wanted. In the hospital she learned that she would be on an equal footing with others who had the same problems and would be treated like everyone else.

Once again, the press was right there reporting her troubles. She issued a press release, hoping the media would get off her back. Instead, as she did for breast cancer, Ford became the "poster child" for recovery from chemical dependence. She was "astonished at the amount of newspaper coverage, the editorials commending my heroism, my candor, my courage. I hadn't rescued anybody from a burning building, I'd simply put my bottles down. It was my family, not I who had been 'candid' and 'courageous'."

But the media had found a star. After her treatment, NBC came in for an interview, despite her protests. "There was no way I should have been put under such pressure," she recalled. "I was upset with my husband, with politics, with everything and everybody. But something good came from that."

The something good Ford is referring to is the Betty Ford Center, which opened at Eisenhower Medical Center in Rancho Mirage in 1982. Working with former ambassador Leonard K. Firestone, who was also recovering, as her co-founder, she raised funds and helped plan what has become perhaps the most outstanding treatment facility in the nation for substance abuse. The board of directors prevailed upon her to use her name, and she serves as a very active chairman of the board of directors.

She has often said that the way she became first lady had been a stroke of fate, God working through her. Similarly she believes that the new chance to help other recovering alcoholics through her own recovery and the foundation of the center was also fate's intervention. For her work, she has become one of America's most honored women, receiving in 1991 the Presidential Medal of Freedom from President George Bush, in addition to many other citations and awards.

Jerry Ford comments: "To have seen the center go from an idea to a successful operation gives [Betty] tremendous satisfaction, particularly to see people come in very sick and leave a few weeks later totally different, healthy, vigorous, with a future ahead of them."

Betty Ford became an American hero by daring to speak honestly about matters others kept secret — cancer and substance abuse. Now, people with these problems everywhere look to her for hope and courage. "By candidly talking about these afflictions," wrote *Forbes* magazine, "she gave numerous people heart to battle their addictions and repair their shattered lives." The magazine noted: "Often greater good is done helping people by private actions rather than by concocting some impersonal government program that too many times helps the bureaucracy more than the beneficiary. Betty Ford's high place in the nation's history is secure."

BETTY FORD'S COUNSEL

"Make plans, but don't project how those plans will turn out. Live in the now, live this minute."

"There are two days we don't have to worry about. One is yesterday, because it is gone, and we can't live it over. The other is tomorrow, because we don't know what it will bring. Today, this day, is all we have, so we should make the best of it."

"We have a civilization that doesn't like to admit nice women drink, a civilization in which the idea of an alcoholic woman's needing special attention is still fairly new."

"Shame and guilt are different. Shame is "I am bad." Guilt is "I have done something bad."

"Addicted people are egocentric babies, and we have to be forced to focus on other people."

"You should not be responsible for the mess an alcoholic makes of his or her life. . . . An enabler's addiction is to the alcoholic."

"You can make it, but it's easier if you don't have to do it alone."

Billy Graham

Billy Graham was dressed in overalls and clod-hoppers. He had just come from his home farm in North Carolina to Wheaton College in Illinois. He was twenty-one years old, feeling like a gangly Li'l Abner, and before him stood Ruth Bell, daughter of a doctor, looking like a slender, brown-eyed movie starlet.

Billy had been helping his friend Johnny Streater that autumn day in 1940, loading a truck with furniture for a lady in a nearby town, when Johnny introduced Billy to the girl of his dreams — the woman who would become his wife. "As far as I was concerned, I just couldn't believe anyone could be as sweet and beautiful as Ruth," Graham, in his mid-seventies, recalled. After a half century of marriage, five children, and nineteen grandchildren, nothing has changed his mind, either.

Ruth and Billy courted by the rules — and then some. They spent Saturday night in prayer and study in preparation for church the next day. They took long walks in the countryside, often stopping to read epitaphs on tombstones. Ruth even asked her parents' permission to wear Billy's engagement ring. She was to become the perfect wife for a man of God.

Billy Graham has courted life as sincerely as he did his wife. He has come to the world just as he is. His innocence, his decency — spoken through his gentle Southern voice — have charmed the world. His manner is so humble and straightforward that people know he believes what he preaches.

He is one of the best respected, most admired, and most trusted individuals in the world. In the past forty years, Graham has been named thirty-three times in the Gallup poll of the Ten Most Admired Men in the World. He has the ability to win and hold the loyalty of people, in part because he focuses his attention entirely on the person he is with, never appearing to be superior or condescending.

He has been heard by hundreds of millions of people in eighty-four countries. He has as much, if not more, influence than the pope. Graham's popularity is so great that there is a gold star on the sidewalk of Los Angeles's Hollywood Boulevard with Graham's name on it, near the stars honoring Frank Sinatra, Tom

Selleck, and Julie Andrews. Someone even once wrote to President Richard M. Nixon to ask that he arrange an interview with Billy Graham.

And yet, Graham has not been corrupted by his success. "The closer you get to most celebrities, the more you are disillusioned," remarked one professor who had worked with Graham on a crusade in England. "With Graham, the closer you get, the more you are impressed."

Graham has also been friends with or personal advisor to each American president since Harry Truman. At practically every swearing-in ceremony, there has been Billy Graham, either simply present or bestowing a benediction. At major turning points in history — such as the decision to go to war with Iraq to liberate Kuwait — Billy Graham was close to the president. Graham eventually came to feel he had been used by some of them to give themselves credibility.

A Southern boy trained in Northern theology, Graham has always been able to bridge differences. Part of his appeal is his belief that doctrine, and even denominations, mean less than personal conversion and holy living. This is why Graham has worked with practically every Protestant group. Even the Roman Catholic church and Billy Graham often find themselves on the same side of a crusade.

Graham was born in Charlotte, North Carolina, and became a dedicated Christian when he was sixteen. He was ordained by the Southern Baptist Convention in 1940 while studying at the Florida Bible Institute. Three years later he was graduated with a degree in anthropology from Wheaton. Since it was the middle of World War II, he joined Youth For Christ and ministered to military personnel. Graham preached throughout the United States and in Europe after the war.

The atheistic world views of Communism and Nazism had led to bloodshed and horror, and millions of people sought to fill the void with a new relationship with God. The world was hungry for meaning and comfort. Bible sales doubled, and people flocked to hear anyone who promised to show the way.

Unfortunately, in that era, "evangelism" meant tent revivals and faith healers; many of the evangelists were the ones Sinclair Lewis amalgamated into the Elmer Gantry stereotype of religious hypocrites of the day. Many fell prey to the very things they preached against, such as sex, greed, and pride.

Graham resolved not to become caught in the trap that ensnared so many others. "Integrity means a man is the same on the inside as he claims to be on the outside," Graham maintains. His success at preserving his own integrity changed the public perception of evangelical Christianity. Because there has always been at least this one man who lives what he believes, he has helped give the religious movement a transfusion.

"It would be difficult to overestimate Billy Graham's importance in the last fifty years of evangelicalism," wrote *Christianity Today.* The magazine said Graham's credibility alone helped many organizations to survive, and those groups in turn have helped millions of people. These include Young Life, Youth for Christ, InterVarsity Fellowship, Campus Crusade, Navigators, and Fellowship of Christian Athletes. At least in some part because of him, one-third of all Americans identify themselves as "born-again" Christians.

The main reason Graham's ministry has withstood the buffeting of the decades is a set of decisions he made when he began his ministry. It was in Modesto, California on a November day in 1948 that Graham called his co-workers, Cliff Barrows, Bev Shea, and Grady Wilson, to his room. Graham told them he believed God Himself had given them success in their ministry, and may be preparing them for even greater service. "Let's try to recall all the things that have been a stumbling block and a hindrance to evangelists in years past, and let's come back together in an hour and talk about it and pray about it and ask God to guard us from them."

None of them was surprised that they each came back with the same list, from which they hammered out the "Modesto Manifesto." The top temptation was money — it was too easy for many of their predecessors to dip into the offerings made by the faithful. That's why Graham resolved to ask members of sponsoring committees to oversee payment of all bills. Graham and his staff receive salaries only, instead of a percentage of the offering. The board of directors of the Billy Graham Evangelistic Association, based in Minneapolis, decides how to spend the money. The directors are mostly successful business people, and Graham is genuinely accountable to them. They sometimes tell him no or to cut back, and he does what they say.

Since sexual immorality had already caused many well-known religious figures to fall from grace, and Graham knew that the mere appearance of impropriety could destroy his credibility, he and his team established rules for themselves that would push temptation far away. They would avoid situations such as meals, sharing a ride, or counseling in which they'd be alone with someone of the opposite sex. When they traveled, they would make it a point to keep their rooms close to one another. And they would always pray for help from God.

There were times when they needed it. A "ladies only" meeting in Portland, Oregon, on a hot August morning in 1950 gathered thirty thousand women, who became so worked up about Graham's visit that they tore down traffic barriers, climbed onto automobiles, and were so rowdy the team had to call the police to keep the women from wrecking the tent.

Graham was an early opponent of segregation. And although blacks had been seated away from whites, separated by ropes at his first crusades, by 1952, when he spoke in Jackson, Mississippi, he was fed up, and pulled down the ropes that kept the races apart. From then on, he insisted that all his crusades be integrated.

"I burned inwardly when once I stopped at a West Coast motel and saw them turning away a Mexican — just because he was a Mexican," Graham once said. "I burned again when on the East Coast, I saw a sign over a restaurant saying: 'Gentiles Only'.

"Can a Christian stand aside and say, 'Let those people suffer those indignities?' Did not Christ say, 'And as you wish that men should do to you, do so to them?' Does the Bible not teach, 'You shall love your neighbor as yourself?' We must enter into their difficulties and problems, and their burdens must be our burdens, if we are to fulfill the law of Christ."

Graham made those remarks in 1956 in *Life* magazine, and that year the governor of South Carolina refused to allow Graham, whom he called "a well-known integrationist," to hold a rally on the grounds of the state capitol. Graham shifted the site to a military base. The sixty thousand people who attended made up the first large-scale gathering of blacks and whites together in the state's history.

The next year, Graham alienated much of his white following when he invited Dr. Martin Luther King, Jr. to come to his crusade. Also in 1957, during his crusade at Madison Square Garden in New York, Graham changed the course of evangelical history by working with mainline and liberal churches — further alienating some of the more sectarian fundamentalists. Never mind. It was the right thing to do, and Graham's followers eventually had to catch up to his position.

They had to adapt to him if they wanted to be part of his work. He simply does too good a job for credible churches to be left out of his ministry. By the time Billy Graham speaks a word at an appearance, there has been months of preparation. His highly professional advance teams have trained local churches so volunteers can help counsel those who have decided to turn their lives over to God. They have rented sometimes hundreds of buses to transport thousands of people to and from arenas and stadiums.

Tens of thousands of people file into the arenas in which Billy Graham is to speak. Always there are smiling volunteers to greet them and help them find seats. Music warms the crowd, and eventually Graham steps forward to the microphone.

His preaching, for the most part, covers a few universal themes, such as sin, redemption, salvation. He speaks clearly and sincerely, and he also grows with the times. In the 1970s and 1980s, for example, he began speaking out on nuclear disarmament, and he has worked for religious freedom throughout the world.

And always the speeches end the same way: Graham invites people to make a decision for God — to get up from their seats and come down front and pray with a counselor. "You come," he says, and millions and millions of people have.

A high point in the career of the evangelist has been bringing his message behind the former Iron Curtain — to those who had been forbidden from hearing it. Moscow's Olympic

Stadium was filled with thirty thousand Christians each day he preached there in 1992. They came from Russia and the Ukraine and Belarus by twelve trains and two hundred buses to hear Graham speak through an interpreter.

"We thought the changes of the past few years had eliminated war, and that we'd have peace throughout the world, and so many of our other problems would be solved," he told the former Soviets. "But we still have disease, we still have poverty, we have hate, we have loneliness, we have boredom, we have unemployment, we have psychological problems . . . and you wonder why. You can come to God tonight. . . . He will fix you and restore you."

In addition to bringing hope, Graham's crusade distributed nearly fifty tons of food and medical supplies in Moscow and other major cities. To keep the momentum in that part of the world, Graham helped teach forty-five hundred Russian religious leaders at the first Moscow School of Evangelism. He was also the first foreign-born evangelist allowed into North Korea.

In the more advanced world, the particular problems are different in kind, but not in nature. "We are finding out that modern technology and science have not solved our problems, have not given us the answers," he says. He often depicts America as a spiritually malnourished nation, despite its great wealth. John Steinbeck, he notes, showed him a letter from Adlai Stevenson that said, "If I wanted to destroy a nation, I'd give it too much."

"That's where America is now, on our knees, greedy sick," Graham says. Only Christians can "totally cope with life and regard death with serenity." Graham speaks with great conviction when he says, "I believe a real spiritual experience with Christ is the answer. It does not mean we won't have problems, but we will have a peace and a joy and a determination to go through those problems with a sense of victory rather than total defeat and despair."

In his latter years, his hands sometimes tremble from advancing Parkinson's disease. It is a condition that worsens over time and destroys brain cells that control muscle movements, leading to an involuntary shaking of the hands and head, and a loss of balance and speech. In some of his appearances, Billy Graham has been helped up and down podium stairs. But he downplays the significance of the disease: "My hand trembles a bit, so I have trouble writing, and after I have walked a mile or so I have a bit of dizziness. But those are the only symptoms." He intends to continue to preach "as long as I have the physical strength, and that depends on the Lord."

Despite being hard pressed by his health, Graham continues to preach at a pace that would exhaust a younger man. To spread hope further, and give people the opportunity to help create hope in others, Graham has collected food at churches and relief organizations for distribution where it is needed. The crusade's Love in Action operation refers thousands of people to local emergency food and shelter programs. Local churches also often organize a resource directory listing human services available through churches.

Crusade organizers maintain that if they do their work right, their efforts represent an opportunity to make each place in which they appear a better place to live.

Graham and his team saw other evangelists lose credibility by exaggerating the sizes of crowds attending their presentations. The bigger the audience, the bigger the ego — and the greater the chance of being invited to preach at bigger churches. Graham doesn't need to boast. He accepts police or fire department crowd size estimates. Over the years, it has become all but impossible to accurately gauge how many people have heard Graham either in person or through broadcasts. The number is certainly well over 100 million —

perhaps that many have heard a single broadcast in Asia alone.

Rising above subjects that are unimportant by eternal standards, Graham refuses to allow his message to become enmeshed with topical issues. When President Bill Clinton was sworn in, for example, militants in the Right-to-Life movement called on Graham to withdraw from participating in the inauguration, but he refused.

He has been pressured from both sides of local controversies to take a position. But he stays above it all. "I will avoid politics. I am here to preach the Gospel. We live in a political season, and there are wonderful people on all sides. I stay out of politics, propositions, and measures. . . ."

Rising above divisiveness is part of what has enabled Graham to help so many people. "We have a larger obligation to serve our neighbors," Graham says. "We need to do God's will in this world." Graham would be pleased if his crusades could help all people learn to love one another, no matter what their differences. That is what God wants and what Christians should aspire to if they want to obey God, he often says.

Billy Graham is a hero because he has stayed true to his principles, never once allowing his own conduct or that of anyone close to him to detract from his message. In the truest sense, he has walked his talk.

ACCORDING TO BILLY GRAHAM

"I don't think this or any other country is going in the right direction. . . . We should be headed in the direction of goodness and righteousness, away from crime and immorality, and toward helping one's neighbors who are in need."

"I believe there is hope for the future. I don't wring my hands and give up. I believe it is possible for us to grapple with the problems of the cities, the nation, and the world and solve them. As long as men and women provide spiritual leadership, there is hope."

"Personal security means knowing and accepting who we are and where we are going. That comes not from careers alone, but from diversifying our emotional portfolio. The only lasting peace and security is of God Himself."

"As Christians we should expect to suffer. It is our calling to deny self and take up the cross and follow Christ."

"Why sin? Why suffering? Why the devil? These are questions I want to ask the Lord when I get to heaven."

Jackie Joyner-Kersee

"Jackie! Jackie!"

The crowd was on its feet in the grandstand, chanting her name. They waved American flags and threw confetti into the bright blue Barcelona sky. They stamped their feet. They whistled. Nothing would satisfy them until she appeared.

"Jackie! Jackie!"

Jackie Joyner-Kersee was tired, but when she heard the chanting, she knew what they wanted.

Jackie emerged from the shadows into the sun-filled stadium, waving to the thousands of fans who had just watched her make history. She had just won the heptathlon (seven events in one sport) in the 1992 Olympics, and by doing so became what some called the sportswoman of the century, and possibly the millennium.

"Jackie! Jackie!"

Jackie couldn't keep herself from grinning. She ran along the grandstand, her taut, ebony five-foot ten-inch body rippling with sinew and muscle and gleaming with sweat. She had just finished running eight hundred meters, throwing javelin and shot put, leaping through the air in the broad jump — seven events altogether — and doing all of it farther and faster than any other woman could.

The grandstand was a sea of outstretched hands — everyone wanted to touch this goddess — and she shook hands with everyone she could reach. They adored her — practically worshiped her.

"You were great, Jackie! You're the best, Jackie! We love you Jackie!"

The adulation came from ordinary people, as well as other celebrities. They called her the all-time greatest multisport athlete of either gender. At one point Bruce Jenner, decathlon champion from 1976, stopped her to say she was "the greatest athlete in the world." The lucrative product endorsement offers poured in. Jackie Joyner-Kersee's image was everywhere. She had it made.

This is heady stuff for anyone to handle. Great achievement and the praises of many can lead to pride, and pride is the enemy of compassion. It would have been so easy for her to go with the flow, to forget her past.

But though the clouds may have beckoned Jackie Joyner-Kersee's head, her feet were too solidly on the ground for her to lose sight of her roots. "I remember where I came from," she says, "and I keep that in mind. . . . If a young female sees the environment I grew up in and sees my dreams and goals come true, she will realize her dreams and goals might also come true."

Joyner-Kersee did not begin life with crowds of worshipers. Far from it. And yet the expectations for her were high from the beginning.

On March 3, 1962, when President John F. Kennedy's wife was the most admired woman in the world and Joyner-Kersee was born in East St. Louis, Illinois, her great-grandmother, Evelyn Joyner, insisted: "Jacqueline! You have to name her Jacqueline!" Why? "Because someday this girl will be the first lady of something."

It was quite a leap of faith to predict such success for this particular baby. She was a healthy enough child, cooing and kicking in her crib, but there were a number of differences between her and her namesake.

This baby was born to teenage, African-American parents. They were married when her father was fourteen and her mother was sixteen, and they were only three years older than that when Joyner-Kersee was born.

The family was anything but rich. Jackie's

mother, Mary Joyner, paid the rent from her pay as a nurse's assistant and from what her husband, Alfred Joyner, Sr., earned in other cities as a construction worker. Later, he worked as a switchman on the railroad, but was still two hours away from their home.

The environment was anything but uplifting. East St. Louis is an old industrial town that is one of the most blighted communities in the country. The Joyner family lived on Piggot Street in a one-story house that was little more than wallpaper and sticks. In winter, the hot-water pipes froze regularly, so the family had to heat their bathwater in kettles on the kitchen stove. Outside, the streets were tough; she saw someone murdered in front of her house when she was eleven years old. Given this unlikely background, was it prophesy, self-fulfilling prophesy, or hope that led Joyner-Kersee's great-grandmother to make such a grand prediction?

But there were bright spots as well. For example, the Mayor Brown Community Center was right across the street from her home. Run by Pop Miles, a man who gave his own time to work with the children, the center was the place she and her friends spent their spare hours. There was an indoor pool and a track as well as activities in which they could participate. There she took dance lessons, and learned that she could run. "I was nine years old when I had my first track competition," she recalls. "I finished last, but the next week in practice, I could feel improvement."

Her mother did not approve. "Track and field — that's not right for a girl," she told her daughter. Her father felt the same way — he frowned and let her know he thought she should quit.

But Joyner-Kersee couldn't seem to stop herself. Her parents watched her running with the other children across the street. And they noticed she was finishing ahead of most of the other kids. She enjoyed running so much and seemed to do so well that they eventually changed their attitude.

The next time Jackie competed, she didn't come in last. She won a second, a third, and a fourth place. The next time she earned three second places. And one day she came home, found her father, and proudly announced: "I got five first places, Daddy."

And she didn't stop with running. She also tried the long jump. By the time she was twelve she could leap seventeen feet. Her older brother, Al, watching his kid sister compete, decided to try it himself and eventually became a track star at Arkansas State and an Olympic competitor himself.

Jackie found that by practicing and trying

hard she could do more than run and jump. She applied herself to her schoolwork with the same dedication. One day when she was in the fifth grade, the teacher explained how to do long division. It didn't make any sense to her when she heard the explanation in class, but she found that if she took the book home and worked it out by herself, she could understand it. Joyner-Kersee worked it out for herself so well she got to sit at the front of the class.

She had plenty of time to put into her schoolwork because her mother refused to permit her to date until she turned eighteen. Seeing her friends going out with boys and having a good time was tempting, but she dared not cross her mother. She resigned herself to the outlets that were available to her — schoolwork and sports.

Joyner-Kersee caught the eye of Pop Miles, who saw that she had Olympic potential. "The quickest way to the Olympics is to master a variety of specialties," he told her. She tried the pentathlon (a sport with five events) and won the National Junior Olympic Championship when she was fourteen. She won the same event every year throughout her career at Lincoln High School, and earned a reputation as one of the finest athletes in the state. She set state records in the long jump, and she played volleyball and basketball.

Her disciplined approach to schoolwork earned her good grades, and she graduated in the top ten percent of her class in 1980. She'd worked hard in her sports, and competed in the U.S. Olympic trials. She had a good chance to represent her country at the games in Moscow, but her efforts were to no avail; that year America boycotted the Olympics to protest the Soviet invasion of Afghanistan.

She would have to wait to show Moscow what she could do. But at least, now that she was eighteen, she could date. And there were opportunities for minority students who excelled academically or athletically. Joyner-Kersee was recruited by the University of California at Los Angeles (UCLA) where she became the star basketball forward.

It was a long way from the slums of East St. Louis to the glitz of Los Angeles, but Joyner-Kersee kept in touch with her family. She was stunned to learn, midway through her freshman year, that her mother had died suddenly of meningitis at the age of thirty-eight.

But when there is a great loss, often there is also an unexpected gain. Her mother's death gave Joyner-Kersee "a clearer sense of reality," she has said. She feels that part of her mother's legacy was her own sense of determination.

Jackie Joyner gained something else at that time: the attention of Bob Kersee, UCLA's assistant track coach, who saw great talent in her. But he also saw she was not getting what she needed to reach her potential as an athlete. Kersee threatened to quit unless he was allowed to coach her. He convinced her to take up the heptathlon, and she qualified for the U.S. Olympic team in 1984, as did her brother, Al, who excelled in the triple jump. Al once said they were both determined to show there were "better things to come out of East St. Louis than just crime."

In the midst of the 1984 Olympics, Joyner-Kersee found herself twenty points behind the leader and with a pulled muscle. Determined to catch up, she thought her long jump would put her ahead, but she did poorly. She took the lead after the javelin throw, but still faced the final event — the eight-hundred-meter run. As she ran the final lap of the race, her brother, Al, ran beside her. "Pump your arms," he shouted. "This is it!" But his encouragement wasn't enough. She missed the gold medal by .06 seconds, while Al himself went on that night to win the triple jump competition.

One of the women Joyner-Kersee competed against, Jane Frederick, had high praise for the athlete from East St. Louis. "Hers was a real talent," Frederick said, "not a forced one. She wasn't driven to compensate for bitterness or character failing."

Even if Joyner-Kersee had won the gold, she still would not have had a shot at the Soviet team. That country and its allies boycotted the Los Angeles Olympics in retaliation for the American boycott in 1980. She didn't get the chance to show them what she could do for another two years.

After four years of working together as coach and athlete, on January 11, 1986 Bob Kersee and Jackie Joyner also became husband and wife. He continued to coach her, working her hard to prepare her for the Goodwill Games in Moscow. (The games were organized by American broadcasting executive Ted Turner, to ease the tension then growing between the United States and the Soviet Union and its allies.)

Jackie Joyner-Kersee was one of the stars of the games. She achieved a personal best record in almost every event, setting a number of records along the way. She was a hit with the Soviets: when she stepped onto the track for the eight-hundred-meter race, the Soviet announcer said in both English and Russian, "We all hope Jackie Joyner will make it." She planned to run it in two minutes and ten seconds, and that is exactly what she did. The announcer lost all objectivity: "It's marvelous! It's magnificent!" he shouted.

She broke the world record by two hundred points, and became the first American woman to hold a multievent world record in fifty years, and the first woman outside the Soviet bloc to do so in a decade.

She was barely rested from Moscow when she competed again, at the U.S. Olympic Festival in Houston, Texas. The temperature rose higher than one hundred degrees, but Joyner-Kersee said, "I just tried to block out all negative thoughts. I kept reading little books I have, books on faith that tell you to just keep exercising your faith and continuing to believe." Her victory gave her the 1986 Sullivan Award, defeating athletes from football and other, better-known sports. She was called "America's greatest athlete since Jim Thorpe."

She won two gold medals in 1988 in Seoul, Korea while setting world records. She injured herself at the 1991 World Championships in the long jump, but came back to again win the Olympic gold medal in 1992 in Barcelona. By the time she had finished the many events of the heptathlon, which seldom draw many spectators, most of the crowd was gone and Joyner-Kersee left the track without taking a victory lap. But the remaining fans chanted her name and wouldn't stop until she made an appearance.

The Women's Sports Foundation named her the Amateur Sportswoman of the year for 1992, and others called her the all-time greatest multisport athlete of either gender. In 1996, she will be thirty-four years old, and expects to compete again in Atlanta. If she succeeds, she'll have achieved another first — no one has ever won a multievent medal at that age. Going into those games, she holds the six highest records in heptathlon history.

In addition, following the 1988 Olympics, she founded the J.J.K. Community Foundation, in order to help young people in urban areas throughout the country realize their potential. (The only 1992 Olympian who was highly successful in terms of endorsements, Joyner-Kersee gives a substantial portion of her endorsement earnings to the foundation, continuing to fund operating expenses.) Her idea is to build "leaders of tomorrow" who can make a difference in the world.

The foundation works with children at elementary, junior high, and high school levels, helping them develop their self-esteem not only through sports, but also through academics, including communications and the arts. The program works in conjunction with compatible community groups, and offers kids adult mentoring as well as scholarships.

Despite all her successes (she has also co-authored a book, *A Woman's Place is Everywhere*, and has hosted television programs on youth issues), Joyner-Kersee has remained the same person she ever was. Someone who has known her for years says, "She is centered, she comes from a very sincere place. Jackie makes you feel comfortable and equal as a human being in the way she treats people and interacts with them."

Nor has she forgotten her roots. Although the foundation has national scope, Joyner-Kersee's first priority is to improve things where she came from: East St. Louis. She gave a five-thousand-dollar scholarship to a National Merit Scholar from her own Lincoln High School. She sends teams of children from her old neighborhood to AAU Junior Olympic Championships. She took one hundred children from her hometown to New York City's Thanksgiving Day Parade. Her commitment to youth in her hometown has even earned her an honorary doctor of law degree from Washington University in St. Louis.

The foundation sponsors a Leadership Awards dinner to acknowledge outstanding people who are role models and leaders in their fields, and who have also given back to the community. Honored individuals include

Winnie Mandela, Coretta Scott-King, Rachel Robinson, and Ruth Owens. The foundation has also honored Martin L. Mathews, who is a community leader and sportsman in St. Louis, Congresswoman Maxine Waters, and Olympic gold medalist Gail Devers. The dinners also serve as fund raisers for the foundation and make the community more aware of its activities. The Leadership Award itself is named after Pop Miles, the man who ran the community center across the street, where Joyner-Kersee got her start as an athlete.

In fact, one of her main goals for the foundation is to restore the Mayor Brown Community Center. Lack of funds forced it to close in the 1980s, and it now stands dilapidated and abandoned. But she is using her persuasive personal skills to line up community support to restore it and reopen it, so that other generations of children can have the same opportunity to compete and grow that she had.

Joyner-Kersee's namesake, Jacqueline Kennedy Onassis, continued to inspire her, even in death. When Mrs. Onassis died from lymphatic cancer, Joyner-Kersee and her husband/coach, Bob, prayed for her. And they dedicated Joyner-Kersee's long jump effort at the New York Games to the former first lady. Joyner-Kersee set a new record.

She speaks of Onassis with the same respect

with which many people speak of her. "She was a role model," Joyner-Kersee says. "Her strength was exemplary. If there's anything I want, it is the strength to endure like she did, to be a classy lady like she was, and to be able to raise children like she did."

JACKIE JOYNER-KERSEE SAYS

"There's more to life than competing. If I can cheer someone on, I'm willing to do that."

"I just tried to block out all negative thoughts. I kept reading . . . books on faith that tell you to just keep exercising your faith and continuing to believe."

"Whatever comes, accept it."

Sammy Lee

Sammy Lee, the first Asian-American to win an Olympic gold medal, was thrilled to bring honor to the United States. The platform diver was also the first Asian-American to win gold medals in two Olympics in a row, and he also became the oldest American to win a gold medal.

But he has earned his status as a hero for helping his country realize — after he eventually did himself — that being an American is a matter of thought and action rather than an issue of skin color. Lee, a Korean-American, had to overcome the obstacle of his own prejudices, even as he led others to overcome theirs. Sammy Lee is a hero for many reasons, but mostly because he helped America live up to its own ideals.

Sammy Lee eyed the new student in his sixth-grade class warily. Until now, he had been the only brown-skinned child in his Highland Park, California school. But now there was another. Lee looked at him across

173

the room full of white faces, wondering.

When Lee's teacher introduced the new boy as Isao Kikuchi, Lee realized his fears were correct . . . the new kid was a Jap, his mortal enemy. The teacher, oblivious to the barrier of nationality between the two Asian boys, assumed Lee would want to be the first to greet the new student. "Perhaps you would like to welcome him, Sammy," he suggested.

On the contrary. Lee resented being singled out. He was annoyed and embarrassed in front of his friends. But mostly, he was angry at what the Japanese had done to his ancestral country — the domination, the exploitation, the executions he had learned about — since they annexed it in 1910. All this seethed in his mind as he slowly walked to the front of the class. Everyone watched as he came near the Japanese boy.

In an instant, Lee's fist flew into the other boy's face, striking him in the mouth. With blood spurting to the floor, the boy stumbled and fell to his seat while Lee glowered over him. The teacher grabbed Lee and threw his tiny frame down. The teacher then dragged him to his feet and ejected him toward the principal's office.

Had the teacher known Sammy Lee as the other kids did, he would have realized how deeply Lee hated the Japanese. He would have heard about the time when, at age four, Lee was taken to a reenactment of the 1919 massacre of Korean students by the Japanese army. Lee's father told him this happened because the Korean students wanted independence. So, the next morning, Lee had burst into the home of Japanese neighbors brandishing a knife and threatening to kill them. But Lee's father told him: "Son, it isn't Mrs. Watanabe, it was the Japanese imperialists who did the killing. Now apologize."

Few other Americans in the 1920s made distinctions among Japanese, Korean, or Chinese ethnicity. Back then, on much of the West Coast, people of all three nationalities were excluded from American citizenship, which is why the deep patriotism many Asian families, such as Sammy Lee's, feel for America is so poignant.

Few people have admired America as much as has Lee's father, Soonkee Rhee. (He changed the family name to Lee in America because people always asked him how to spell Rhee.) He was born in Seoul, Korea and grew up close friends with Syngman Rhee, who later became president of South Korea. Soonkee Rhee hated the rigid discipline of the Buddhist school he attended. When Syngman Rhee told him about America and the freedom and opportunity that came from people making their own decisions in a democracy, Soonkee Rhee wanted to go there.

He got his opportunity by working as an interpreter for an American company building a railroad in Korea. The workers were so impressed with his interest in America that they took up a collection to send him there, and to Occidental College in Los Angeles. Here, his love of America led him to renounce his Buddhist upbringing and become a Christian.

When Japanese oppression became unbearable in Korea, Lee sent for his wife, Eunkee, who was the first Korean woman to emigrate to the United States. After having daughters Dolly and Mary, she gave birth to Samuel on August 1, 1920. His sisters called him Sammy because that sounded more American.

To support his family, Lee dropped out of Occidental and gave up his dream of becoming an engineer in order to farm in the San Joaquin Valley. He received an occasional threat because of his race, but believed so strongly in the American ideal of opportunity that he did not falter. Lee refused to accept welfare, although he had fewer possessions than many who did. He believed in standing on his own feet, and he supported the government's policies.

At the time, there were so few Koreans in this country that there was no pejorative term for them. It was ironic that Sammy Lee would later hold so much hatred against the Japanese; most Americans thought he *was* Japanese, calling him "Jap" or "Chink" for lack of better words.

He first heard such abuse when he was seven years old. After a day at school, a little girl invited him to her home to play. The girl skipped through the kitchen door with Lee, the smallest child in the class, right behind her. His easy smile won him many friends in class, but could not melt the little girl's mother. She frowned at him.

"Get that Chink out of here before I count to three," the woman insisted to her daughter, "or you'll know the reason why." Lee felt the woman's hostility and ran to his father's store, from then on staying away from his friends' homes.

"What is a Chink, Papa?" he asked. Lee had been busy taking care of customers, but he stopped to answer his son. He explained to him that the word meant a Chinese person, and that like Chinese and Japanese, Koreans are Orientals. But he also explained that having origins outside America was not a matter of shame.

"It is something to be proud of," Lee told his son. "America is made up of people from all over the world — Germans, Englishmen,

Irish, Swedes, Dutch, Spanish, Italians, Indians, Africans, Hindus, and so on. This is the melting pot of the world, and it is producing the finest civilization on Earth. Be proud that you are a part of it, my son."

Because the elder Lee believed so strongly in America, he was especially disappointed when he learned his son hated the Japanese. Lee told his son that he was being prejudiced against the Japanese the way other people were against him. "A Christian does not hate people," his father told him. "Ideas, actions, but never people."

The youngest Lee soon showed himself to be wiry and strong, independent and hard to control. He was thrown out of one school because he was a discipline problem, and a Catholic school refused to accept him because of his reputation. Recognizing that his uncontrolled behavior would hold him back even more than the shade of his skin would, Lee's father taught the boy the need to be responsible for his actions. "Self-discipline is not allowing yourself to do anything you may later regret, and making yourself do everything that may help you grow," he said. "Sometimes it is not easy. If you are successful at disciplining yourself, you will develop self-esteem and you will be happy with yourself."

One day Lee made a discovery that changed

his life. He noticed that the most respected children at his school (he had asked to go to a reform school because he had seen the boys out in the field playing and being active) were those who excelled in sports. Though he was the smallest person in class, he was also one of the most energetic and coordinated.

And he discovered that he loved to dive. This was the perfect sport for his agility, speed, and bravado. The Brookside Park Pool allowed nonwhites to swim on Mondays only, and that became Lee's favorite day of the week. With his natural agility, he leapt from the board and somersaulted in the air before entering the water. Before long, he was improvising his own dives.

One day in 1932, Lee saw hundreds of flags from many nations all over Los Angeles. He learned from his father that the flags were for games in which athletes had the chance to bring honor to their countries as well as themselves by proving themselves to be the greatest athletes in the world.

"Papa, I, too, want to be an Olympic champion," Lee said. His father chuckled and asked, "Which sport?"

"I don't know, but I'll find it," he replied. Whichever sport it turned out to be, it would have to be one suitable for a short person: he never grew beyond five feet one inch. It would have to be a sport that rewarded courage, intelligence, and discipline.

Although Lee was good at football and tumbling — he even became a cheerleader — he excelled in diving. He won city championships, but needed coaching to reach his full potential. A friend and fellow diver, Hart Crum, who was an African-American, coached him as best he could. Nonetheless, some of the other kids at the pool teased him because of his color.

"I may look like an Oriental, but I'm an American," Lee shouted at them. "I can do anything you can do, and I'm going to prove it." It was that anger, and the desire to do better than a Japanese-American boy a year ahead of him, that motivated Lee.

When he complained to his father about the discrimination against him, his father showed him a different perspective: "There will always be bigots prejudiced against you," he told Lee, "especially when you succeed in accomplishing something where they have failed. You must not let anything they say or do discourage you. Rather, continue to improve yourself and let your native heritage reflect your strengths. With your own dignity unimpaired, others will automatically respect you."

One day when Lee was practicing, famed

Olympic coach Jim Ryan noticed him. "See that Chink over there?" Ryan said to Hart Crum. "I'm going to make him the greatest diver in the world, or kill him. I'm going to work a miracle. I'm going to show the world that even a runt of a Chink can become a champion."

Ryan humiliated and degraded Lee, browbeat him and drove him to exhaustion. Ryan was the most negative and prejudiced man Lee had ever met, but the most knowledgeable in diving mechanics. Lee put up with it because Jim Ryan was the answer to his prayers. Through this rude man, Lee knew he could become an Olympic champion.

Lee also knew that despite his coarse words, Ryan had faith in him — so much faith he was serving as his coach with no financial reward. Ryan once told Lee: "I saw you had a lot of spunk, Sammy, and unless an athlete has that, he'll never be a winner." Ryan also told him: "There can be no mediocrity for a winner. Never forget it."

Lee wondered why this man of many prejudices would spend his own time coaching him. Until he talked with Farid Simaika, an Egyptian diver who, coached by Ryan, had won an Olympic gold medal, only to see it stripped away on a technicality. Simaika told him that Ryan had vowed to someday return with an unbeatable nonwhite diver, yearning to humble the judges who, Ryan believed, had cheated him. "You, Sammy, are that diver," Simaika explained, "and you must do dives that the world has not seen, and you must be forty points better than the rest."

Lee continued to win many diving awards, often with dives he had invented. And he was also doing well in high school: he was an A student, became valedictorian of his class, was chosen student body president, and won the school's Alumni Award. "Papa, you were right," he told his father. "In America anything is possible."

Once, after a diving meet, he mentioned to his father that the judges had not been fair to him. His father said, "Promise me that you will never cry discrimination because of losing. Make yourself better and better and some day you will be a winner because you never made excuses when you lost. Every defeat is a lesson for eventual victory."

When his application to UCLA was brushed aside, he always believed it was for racial reasons. But he was accepted at Occidental College, the same small, liberal arts school his father and older sisters attended, and was awarded a full scholarship.

Although his father died before Lee had the chance to compete in the Olympics (the 1940 games were canceled because of the war), he did have the satisfaction of seeing at least one of his goals for Lee come true. At a diving meet in Columbus, Ohio, Lee met a young man, Keo Nakama, he believed to be Japanese. Nakama felt Lee's hostility, and confronted him:

"I want to be friendly with you, Sammy Lee. I consider you a great athlete and I have observed your warm nature. Yet I think you dislike me."

Embarrassed as he was, Lee confessed that he hated the Japanese.

"I am not Japanese, I am Okinawan," Nakama said. "But that is not the issue, as I see it. I believe you blame Japanese-Americans for what the Japanese nation is doing. Then you are doing what others are doing to you. We are all Americans."

Lee looked at this young man with fresh eyes. He felt ashamed of his own mean and petty prejudices and extended his hand in friendship. Nakama eventually became a state legislator in Hawaii and was a world-record swimmer.

Lee told his father he had done well in the competition, but more important, had mastered his own prejudice. "What takes a long time in developing eventually becomes perfect," his father replied.

During World War II, Lee saw many Japanese-Americans, including Isao Kikuchi, the boy he had hit in the face, taken away to internment camps. Many Koreans wore buttons that said: "I am Korean, Not a Jap" to keep from being swept away with them. Although he, too, wore one, Lee took his off when he realized that it could just as easily have been him losing his rights as an American.

Ever since he had an earache as a child, Lee wanted to become a doctor, but his premedical advisor at Occidental would not recommend him for medical school because he was too sports-minded. But when Lee's father passed away, the advisor relented out of respect and made the recommendation. In 1942 Lee joined the U.S. Army Reserves and was accepted to medical school at the University of Southern California. He had such difficulty in medical school that he failed many classes and was advised to drop out. Word of his impending failure traveled quickly through the Korean community, and Lee realized he was about to bring shame upon his family.

But he would not give up. He knew he always came through when the pressure was on. The self-discipline his father had taught him paid off. He joined a group of students who studied together, worked hard, never missed a class or lecture, was punctual and organized, and managed to bring up his grades.

Lee became somewhat of a symbol to the medical students. When another medical student failed a test, he was reminded that Sammy Lee had made it against great odds. Lee's name became synonymous with success in the face of adversity. Later in life, he felt blessed that his life had not been an easy one, believing that he had grown because of the hardships — perhaps even achieved all that he had because of them.

So he could have enough time to be class president, Lee's classmates even offered to cheat for him. But he refused: "I'm going to do it myself," he vowed. Besides, what if he had a patient whose life depended on his knowing what to do? What good would the cheating do him then?

Lee was graduated from medical school in June 1946 and fulfilled his commitment to the army. He noticed that many of the same people who offered to cheat for him, now that their educations were finished, found excuses rather than complete their obligations to their country.

Lee was relieved of his duties as an army doctor so he could train full-time for the 1948 Olympics in England. His drive to succeed in medical school followed through in sports, and he won a bronze medal in the three-meter springboard contest, with the platform competition yet to come. He learned that his race had become an issue with some judges, and he was more determined than ever to succeed.

From high atop the ten-meter platform, the pool below seems very small. By the time a diver hits the water, he is going fast enough to break bones and even die if he does the dive wrong. Lee was keyed up with a dangerous mix of emotions — fear and anger, pride and determination. He had done every dive perfectly so far. He sprang into the air for his final dive. If he could just complete his three-and-one-half forward somersault, the most difficult and dangerous dive in his arsenal, he could have the gold medal.

When his head popped out of the water, he heard the cheers and saw the scores. He had done it!

With the ribbon of victory around his neck, Lee became a sports hero and somewhat of a celebrity. He had stayed away from girls while he was in training, not wanting to be distracted from practice, letting it be known that he had never found a girl short enough to marry. Now he was deluged with offers. Lee enjoyed the attention, but wanted to get back to practicing medicine. "To be able to relieve pain and to heal an ailing body — to me there is nothing to compare with it," he explains.

Lee went to the 1952 Olympics in Helsinki, Finland, where he gave himself a present for his thirty-second birthday: his victory made him the oldest man ever to win the ten-meter competition, the first man to win the Olympic gold medal in high tower diving twice in a row, and the first Asian-American to win the gold, not once, but twice. It was the first time since the war that Germany and Japan competed.

Lee went on a world tour, representing the United States as a goodwill ambassador. He spoke to large groups of important people about America and democracy, and there were frequent headlines, such as the one in Singapore: "Oriental represents America."

After Lee dove with the Japanese team in Tokyo in 1953, they asked for his help. They told him they thought a diver had to be white to win a gold medal, but after seeing him do it, hoped they might also have a chance. Lee took Toshio Ohtsubo, later an international diving judge, and his wife, Keiko Osaki, an Asian Games champion, into his home as guests. After the 1964 Olympics, the Japanese diving team stayed with him.

In the late fifties, Lee began coaching. When Bob Webster came to him, Lee put it to him in plain words: "It will be hours of work, every day, every weekend, month in, month out, clean living, good food, rest, all things I will prescribe for you. The point is," Lee asked, "are you willing to make this one thing your goal, sacrificing everything else when necessary, just to keep your eye on the end result?"

Webster accepted Lee's discipline, and duplicated his feat of winning back-to-back gold medals, in 1960 and 1964. Greg Louganis also worked with Lee, living in Lee's home for months prior to the 1976 Montreal Games at which he won a silver medal. Louganis's next coach, Ron O'Brien, thanked Lee after Louganis's 1984 success (he won two gold medals), and said he should take some credit for it.

Despite the glory and honor Lee brought to the United States in sports, he feels it was on the home front that he has done the greatest good. After his 1952 victory, he and his wife, Chinese-American Roz Wong, set out to buy a house in southern California. But even though he had served his country in the military, helped people get well as a doctor, won Olympic gold medals for America, and represented his country on a goodwill tour, there were places he was not permitted to live.

When the word got out, the story appeared simultaneously in the *San Francisco Chronicle* and on CBS News. From there, his name was all over major newspapers across America. He got messages of support from President Dwight Eisenhower, Vice President Richard Nixon, even television celebrity Ed Sullivan. As a result of Lee's moral courage, a human rights commission was formed that ended exclusionary real estate practices in southern California.

"At last I am doing something for my country," Lee told friends at the hospital where he worked. "My father would have considered this the most important act of a man's life, striking a blow for freedom."

SAMMY LEE'S ADVICE

"Your desire to be a champion must be greater than your fear of failure."

"When you lose a competition, remember: 'Disgusted but never discouraged.'"

"Defeats and disappointments are necessary to build a firm, strong foundation that will hold the burden of your success."

"Everyone cannot become a gold medalist, but you are a failure if you don't try."

"The wise use of freedom is what has made America great."

"We of foreign blood must always do our best for America. She has already given us so much."

"I have faith in America to do the right thing. And you must not forget that in the end, right will triumph."

Antonia Coello Novello

"Toñita" Coello spent a lot of time in hospital beds in Fajardo and San Juan, Puerto Rico in the early 1950s. Born with megacolon, a congenital condition characterized by an enlarged, malfunctioning intestine, suffering was nothing new to her. Every year it was the same for the little girl — every year her stomach swelled up, and every year she wound up in the hospital.

There, the doctors "cleaned her up," as she later put it, and sent her back home. "I was hospitalized every summer for at least two weeks. My pediatrician and my gastroenterologist were so nurturing and good to me that doctors became my buddies," she recalls. One of her favorite nurses was also her aunt, who used to whisper to her as she lay in bed: "Toñita, you should become a doctor yourself."

The only solution to her medical condition, she learned when she was eight years old, was to operate. But she became one of those people who "fall through the cracks" in the medical system, as she puts it, and didn't undergo the surgery she required until more than ten years later.

But Dr. Antonia Coello Novello, former surgeon general of the United States, as well as the first woman and the first Hispanic person to have held the position, is a master at finding a positive light to shine on misfortune. From having spent so much time in hospitals in order to overcome a chronic illness, grew her determination that "no other person would have to wait eighteen years for corrective surgery."

In addition, her aunt's encouragement and the gentle kindness of her pediatrician made her want to become more like them — to care for others in the same way. "My childhood gastroenterologist later on in my life became the dean of the medical school that I attended, and all my life, his was the hand I saw — soothing and caring."

Those combined factors account for the fact that she became "a woman in whom Mother Teresa meets Margaret Thatcher," describes her husband, Joseph. It is a very apt description: she has a compassionate heart for all children like Mother Teresa, and the fighting spirit of the former British prime minister, Margaret Thatcher. She will be remembered as perhaps the most ardent defender of children's health the country has ever had.

In the summer between Antonia Coello's sophomore and junior years in college — she was a biology major at the University of Puerto Rico in Rio Piedras — she told her mother she was determined to have the surgery she required. "By the time I was eighteen," she recalls, "it was not good to have those big bellies one month, and gone flat belly the next."

Even though the little town they lived in was thirty-two miles from the University of Puerto Rico Medical School Hospital and no particular doctor was in charge of her medical follow-up, she believed she could have the operation during the summer break and then live a normal life, free of embarrassingly big bellies and annual hospital stays.

In the absence of a known surgeon, the only person willing to give the operation a try was a cardiovascular surgeon. He did his best, but there were complications from the procedure. Eventually she went to the Mayo Clinic where all the complications were corrected.

"God bless my doctor at the Mayo," she said many years later. There she learned first-hand about the relationship between the cared for and the care giver. She learned that patients do not like to be treated as objects —

that children, especially, like a doctor who will take time to play or talk with them or bring them a magazine. "I know it's the good doctors who come into your room and talk to you like a human being . . ." she said at the time.

A lifetime of illness, losing one's father in childhood, poor results of surgery, and undergoing other operations would have caused many others to give up. But Antonia Coello, characteristically, chose the opposite: "I have no patience for self-pity. Life issues you a card, and you have to learn to play it."

In this she had an excellent example from her mother who, after her husband's death, also could have given up. Instead, she provided the girl with an impressive role model. Her mother spent more than fifty years as a teacher and then a middle school principal in their little town in Puerto Rico. She was even her daughter's seventh grade math and science teacher.

"All my life, I've seen my mother studying," Novello remembers. "She started out as a teacher with a two-year college education. Then she took her bachelor's degree, then her master's. So, I've always thought that in order to succeed, you must work in stages, carefully preparing for each. But more important, my mother felt that education was the key to a better life, and she pushed my brother and me to do our very best."

In 1965, Antonia Coello obtained her bachelor of science degree, but had learned more in college than her professors had taught her. After her first bowel surgery, she had to wear diapers to class for six months, a humbling experience. "I hope this is not arrogance, but experience," she said. "If I can come back from my second surgery and go to college wearing Pampers for six months, I know that nothing is going to pull me down. When I was in college with Pampers on I used to laugh by myself thinking, 'If only they knew.' I survived many times in my life by learning to laugh at myself — that's the best medicine."

But having faced that obstacle and succeeding despite it, she realized, "If I could do that, I can do anything." She learned that even the worst medical problems need not necessarily stop people from accomplishing their goals. Twenty years of her own illness left her little tolerance for people who complain of pain they don't really have, "or who use sickness as their piggyback for not doing what they are supposed to do. And I have very little tolerance for people who say they can't do something or they can't get to the top because of perceived difficulties along the way. Believe me, if I did it . . . it can be done."

Upon receiving her undergraduate degree, she applied to the university's medical school in San Juan. But she did not tell her mother until after she was accepted, "because of the typical attitude of women at that time — fear of failure. There were only sixty-five people per class."

She wasn't sure how she would pay for this opportunity, "but Mommy never panicked. When I told her I was accepted to medical school she said that as long as there is a bank out there we will find your tuition." She earned her medical degree in 1970, the same year she married Joseph Novello, a flight surgeon in the U.S. Navy.

The couple moved to Ann Arbor, Michigan, where they both went on for more medical training at the University of Michigan Medical Center. Novello accepted an internship and two-year residency in pediatrics and her husband studied psychiatry. She did so well that she was named Intern of the Year in 1971.

But the pleasure of being so honored soon wore off: her aunt, the aunt who had urged her to become a doctor, died of kidney failure, and Novello herself was hospitalized with a severe kidney problem as well. As she recovered, she decided to specialize in kidney diseases so that no one in her family would ever go undiagnosed. She took advanced kidney studies both at the University of Michigan Medical Center and at Georgetown University Hospital in Washington, D.C.

In 1976, Novello decided to try pediatrics and opened a private practice in Springfield, Virginia. But she realized after two years that she felt idle taking care of one patient and one disease at a time, when there was so much to be done, so much to learn. Many times she'd cry over the sick children as much as their parents did. "When the pediatrician cries as much as the parents do, then you know it's time to get out," she observes.

Around the same time, much to her and her husband's disappointment, she had to have an emergency hysterectomy. Yet, ever the optimist, Novello found a positive way to view the reality of not being able to bear children. "Not having children probably has helped because I don't feel so torn between kids who are at home and taking care of all the kids out there. More importantly, all of them have become my own and, as such, it is my responsibility to care for them."

After leaving private practice in 1978, she thought of joining the navy, but instead was hired as a project officer in the artificial kidney program with the United States Public Health Service at the National Institutes of Health. She earned a master's degree in public health at the Johns Hopkins University School of Public Health in Baltimore, Maryland, in 1982, and served as a legislative fellow assigned to work with the U.S. Senate. Through a Senate committee, she helped draft and enact the National Organ Transplant Act of 1984, which made it possible for many Americans to receive organ transplants that would have been impossible otherwise.

It was as a legislative fellow that Novello struck her first — but certainly not her last — blow against an enemy of children: tobacco. She helped draft warning labels to be used on cigarette packages and elsewhere, which told of the health risks associated with smoking.

In 1986, she was named deputy director of the National Institute of Child Health and Human Development. There, she coordinated pediatric AIDS research. She thought she had gone as far in her career as she could go, but in 1989, President George Bush nominated her to become the fourteenth surgeon general of the United States. Because of her twelve years of experience in public health and her personal dedication, her nomination progressed through confirmation hearings before the Senate Committee on Labor and Human Resources without major problems.

When she was sworn in on March 9, 1990,

in the Roosevelt Room of the White House, she said: "The American Dream is alive and well today. I might say today the *West Side Story* comes to the West Wing."

In her first year on the job, she listened and studied the American scene. She often visited young patients in hospitals, hugging and nurturing wherever she could. Her philosophy was that bureaucracy should be made easy, and her motto was "good science and good sense." She felt that she could remove fear — she decorated her office with Cabbage Patch dolls, quilts dedicated to AIDS patients, and photos of children and their artwork — open doors, teach, and therefore help others. "I know that if I make good sense and I'm understood, people might be willing to make some good changes." She felt that in the long run, she would be more effective if her messages were easily understood. And to use her position as a "bully pulpit" most effectively, she picked her topics carefully.

Alcohol advertising was among the first issues to draw her fire. She said it often "misleads, misinforms, and unabashedly targets youth." At a press conference in 1991, she said alcohol advertising featured sports heros and other people who are "physically appealing, strong, attractive to the opposite sex, and generally seem to have the best of things going for them." She complained that the advertisements "make drinking look like the key to fun and a wonderful and carefree life-style." Those that showed risky activities, such as mountain climbing, surfing, and skiing, which seem to imply that it is safe for people to drink while involved in these activities, especially incensed her.

In her attacks, she cited a 1990 survey conducted by the National Institute on Drug Abuse that found that about forty percent of college students, thirty-eight percent of tenth graders, and twenty-six percent of eighth graders had five or more drinks on a single occasion in the two weeks preceding the poll. "The typical college student spends more money for alcohol than for books," she said.

She acknowledged that it would require a "societywide partnership" including parents, schools, communities, law enforcement agencies, and governments to combat youthful drinking. But her main recommendation was that the alcohol industry voluntarily give up advertising that targeted youth.

Next, to get her point about the dangers of smoking across to young people, she set her sights on one of the most visible targets imaginable: the R. J. Reynolds tobacco company's Joe Camel cartoon character. The smoking camel figure had become as recognizable as Mickey Mouse to children as young as six through a multimillion-dollar advertising campaign. Novello believed the campaign was intended to create a new generation of smokers to fill the ranks emptied by the 434,000 who die each year as a result of smoking-related disease.

Novello was concerned that every day more than three thousand preteens and teenagers began smoking. She knew that ninety percent of adult smokers began as children or teenagers. Novello predicted that at the current rate of increase in smoking, at least five million children then alive in America would eventually die of smoking related diseases.

She was also concerned about women. She knew that by the last half of the 1990s, women could be smoking at a higher rate than men. "It is tragic . . . that lung cancer has surpassed breast cancer as the number-one cause of death in women," she says. "Call it a case of the Virginia Slims woman catching up with the Marlboro Man."

So, at a March, 1992, news conference, she stood beside James S. Todd, executive vice president of the American Medical Association, to urge R. J. Reynolds to withdraw its advertising campaign. It was a bold, dramatic way to call attention to the problem. Every surgeon general since 1961 had warned

Americans about the dangers of smoking, but singling out such a highly visible ad campaign to attack brought the point home to many.

Domestic violence — especially violence directed at women — is another public health issue she addressed. Such violence is "a cancer that gnaws at the body and soul of the American family," she proclaimed, observing that it is "the second most common cause of injury among women overall, and the leading cause of injuries to women ages fifteen to forty-four. It is more common than automobile accidents, muggings, and rapes combined."

And the bad habits of the fathers are passed along to the sons. "Far too often boys who witness parental violence are more likely, as adults, to be abusive to their partners than are men who did not observe domestic violence when they were children." Unfortunately, she found, the issue of domestic violence did not attract as captive an audience as had abuse of tobacco and alcohol.

She also used her position to call attention to the sagging support of child vaccination against common infectious diseases, as well as the lack of proper prenatal care. Issuing warnings and reports about the danger of the rapid spread of AIDS among America's young people was also high on her priority list.

Novello's concern for children also extended into the nation's agricultural sphere. One out of five farm deaths involves a child under the age of sixteen, and the death rate in agriculture overall is almost five times that of all other industries combined. Consequently, she convened the first surgeon general's occupational conference in fifty years, gathering 650 safety specialists and health care professionals together at Farmsafe 2000 to focus on health problems in agriculture.

Novello's concern for minorities led her to launch the National Hispanic-Latino Health Initiative, which for the first time would address health problems specific to this group. Under her guidance, forty-eight Hispanic-Latino health professionals of the executive planning committee held a national conference in 1992.

Currently, Novello serves as United Nations Children's Fund (UNICEF) Special Representative for Health and Nutrition, for women, children, and youth. In this position, she provides leadership for efforts to immunize the world's children, prevent illegal underage use of tobacco, and eliminate iodine deficiency.

As she reflects on her term as surgeon general, she says: "I'd like to be able to say: 'Kids got vaccinated because we worked on it. Underage drinking was at least thought about much more comprehensively. Research began targeting women as well as men.' I'd also like to be able to look back over my term in office and see that somewhere along the way women stopped smoking — if not for themselves, then for their children."

Why is it so important to her to have done so much for others? "I want to be able to look back someday and say, 'I did make a difference.' Whether it was to open the minds of people to think that a woman can do a good job, or whether it's the fact that so many kids out there think that they could be me, then all the headaches . . . will have been worth it."

ADVICE FROM
DR. ANTONIA COELLO NOVELLO

"Build on what you are to become somebody."

"I survived many times in my life by learning to laugh at myself — that's the best medicine."

"Dreams sometimes come true in strange ways."

"The American Dream is no abstraction to me. I've lived it."

"Having been born with a congenital defect makes me think that everything has a chance to live."

"We all have to demonstrate responsible behavior. It has to start in the home, but it must follow in the school."

"Don't dwell on the negative. If you think a goal is unattainable . . . it probably will be."

Colin Powell

The parades are over, the cheering crowds are silent, and the title — chairman of the Joint Chiefs of Staff — is gone. Yet Colin Powell, the first African-American ever to hold the highest position in United States fighting forces, has shown that heroism comes as much from being the peacemaker as from victory on the battlefield.

He has been described as a symbol of reconciliation. Colin Powell has helped to heal the wounds of the racial unrest, as well as those of the Vietnam War, that racked the nation in the 1960s. Even more, he has proven that the rules of the game in this country are universal, and that anyone who plays by them can rise to the top.

Powell has earned his place in history as the military leader who brought America and the Allied coalition one of the most lopsided victories of all time: the 1991 liberation of Kuwait from Iraq in a hundred-hour, lightning war.

He was militarily responsible for the 541,000 American service personnel who were deployed to the Persian Gulf, and coordinated the efforts of tens of thousands of Allied combatants. He let the generals in the field handle the details of the war plan, and served as the liaison to the president, the secretary of defense, and the National Security Council. He sold the strategies to the national leaders, and had the information they needed in order to be able to make sound decisions. President George Bush counted on him and placed his trust in him.

When another tense situation developed, in Haiti a few years later, Powell's conquest was with words — not weapons. Haitian dictator Raoul Cedras — a proud man — had declared he would rather die fighting American intervention in his country than at the hands of his defeated, occupied people. Yet Powell, along with former president Jimmy Carter and Senator Sam Nunn, persuaded Cedras to avoid war and allow democracy to return to that country.

Cedras's wife had vowed that she and her children would die with her husband. But Powell took her aside and privately convinced her that her husband's honor would be higher, that his courage would be more revered, for stepping aside and preventing bloodshed. It was the right thing to do for Haiti, but it took a respected American military man with a similar background to convince the Haitian junta.

Powell — the son of Jamaican immigrants Luther and Maud Powell — was born in New York City's Harlem, and grew up in the South Bronx with a strong, extended family surrounding him. His grandmother, who everyone knew as "Miss Alice," lived with them, as did other relatives. His oldest sister, Marilyn Powell Burns, says, "We were never alone; we were always closely supervised." Neighbors kept close tabs on the behavior of each other's children, so that young people had the feeling of "all these eyes watching."

Because of this social support, the children grew up with a strong sense of security. One of his cousins, James Watson, a federal judge from New York, has said all of Powell's honors "arose from family roots. That's what Colin is all about."

Because of his Jamaican heritage and culture, Powell could address his experience in American society unfettered by the heritage of slavery. He has no sense of himself as a victim nor a belief "that somebody owes him something," his cousin says.

With fresh eyes, he explored the streets of the South Bronx, and got to know people of many cultures. His playmates were the Jews, Italians, Poles, and other immigrants who shared the vast, crowded city with him.

Powell learned through working after school and during vacations at Sickser's, a furniture store, that hard work alone is the key to success.

At the age of sixteen, in early 1954, he became a freshman at City College of New York. It wasn't that he was enthusiastic about higher education, but that his mother convinced him that engineering was his route to financial success. He switched majors to geology and struggled through college until he found something that inspired him: ROTC.

"I had a certain interest in the military," he recalls. His generation had grown up with the heroism of World War II and then the Korean conflict. "So, if you were of that generation, the military made an indelible impression on you." He came out of college with a degree, a commission as a second lieutenant, and a future.

He went into the military in 1958, at a time when the barriers of segregation were beginning to fall in his own country, and when the world was polarized into the Cold War. He excelled in the military, served two tours of duty in Vietnam, and was promoted to lieutenant colonel.

Next he went to Washington, D.C. to work at the Pentagon. At the age of thirty-one, he was working for the number-three officer there, General William E. Dupuy. At the same time, he earned a master's degree in business administration at George Washington University.

In 1972, he applied for a White House Fellowship. White House Fellows are young professionals, such as military officers, lawyers, business people and others interested in the political process, who spend a year working with the executive branch of government. Out of more than one thousand applicants, Powell was one of 130 invited for interviews and was one of thirty-three national finalists.

For three and a half days, he and the other finalists were interviewed and inspected. Powell was one of two African-Americans among the seventeen fellows selected. He was thirty-six at the time — one of the oldest chosen. One of the other fellows once said of Powell: "He helped other people with the perspective of what was important and what was not. He was a nice guy, a consensus builder. All the things people write about him now, they were there then."

Because Powell had earned his master's in business administration, he was assigned to work at the Office of Management and Budget, where he met a group of individuals whose influence was destined to increase. Caspar Weinberger, for example, headed the OMB, and his deputy was Frank Carlucci. Both of these men eventually became secretary of defense.

Powell told the *Los Angeles Times* in 1991 that being a White House Fellow was "a defining experience." It was there that he learned the function of compromise and consensus, of public relations, and how to handle the media, which helped in his rise to power in the military.

After his stint at OMB, he volunteered for a tour of duty in Korea so that he could have the experience of commanding a battalion. There, his skills with people enabled him to harmonize a tense situation between racial groups.

When Powell came back to Washington in 1974, he was selected to attend the National War College at Fort McNair, where Powell learned about the philosophy of warfare. He learned that warfare is fraught with uncertainties and that commanders operate with information that is never complete. He also learned that ultimately, the moral strength of leaders and soldiers is what leads to victory.

Powell became a colonel, went back into active service for fifteen months, and then back to

Washington. Within two years, he was asked to become senior military assistant to Deputy Secretary of Defense Charles Duncan, who chose Powell because of his reputation for working extremely well with people, being a fast learner, and having great energy and stamina.

Powell became a general, and when Ronald Reagan entered the White House, Powell's star continued to rise. His old associates, Weinberger and Carlucci offered him new opportunities. He became the fourth African-American to achieve the rank of four-star general and the first to serve as chairman of the Joint Chiefs of Staff.

Powell built a solid foundation of trust among the African-American community by his conduct during the Gulf War. Although they represent twelve percent of the nation's population, African-Americans comprise twenty-five percent of the military and by some reports accounted for thirty percent of the troops present in the Persian Gulf.

Because of this, Powell had to face down criticism when fourteen members of the Congressional Black Caucus, along with staff and security personnel, squared off with him around a U-shaped table. Some feared a shouting match, considering the Black Caucus's opposition to the conflict overseas. They saw African-American participants in the American military as mercenaries for rich white families.

But Powell presented his views with sensitivity. He explained why so many African-Americans were taking part in the operation. He patiently showed the caucus members that many African-Americans joined the military because of the travel, educational, and vocational training benefits. He showed a film of interviews with African-American troops, both men and women, who offered no criticism of their military experience.

"I wish there were other activities in our society and in our nation that were as open as the military is to upward mobility, to achievement, to allowing them in," Powell once told Congress. "I wish that corporate America, I wish the trade unions around the nation, would show the same level of openness and opportunity to minorities that the military has. That's why I came in. To get a job."

But the most convincing thing he did was to win the war quickly, decisively, and for the most part, painlessly. Instead of seeing the cream of America's young people return in body bags, as had a previous generation, the country saw them return as heroes. And because African-Americans participated disproportionately in the Gulf War effort, Powell raised the importance of the entire African-

American community.

And that is something he has long fought to do. Through his career in the military, he has worked to reclaim the dignity, lost by years of neglect, of African-American service personnel. When he was deputy commander of Fort Leavenworth, Kansas, in 1982, he worked to erect a monument on the post to the Buffalo Soldiers, the first all-African-American regiments to formally serve in the U.S. Army.

Formed shortly after the Civil War from the highly-successful U.S. Colored Troops, which fought alongside Union forces, the Buffalo Soldiers were given their name by the Native American tribes they fought (the Cheyenne, the Apache, and the Sioux) because of their dusty blankets, their brave fighting, and the resemblance of their coiled hair to the buffalo's. They became one of the most highly decorated groups in American military history and received a total of twenty-four Medals of Honor and many other citations over the years. Although they fought under a veil of anonymity over the years, they maintained one of the lowest desertion records and best combat records in the U.S. Army.

African-American regiments went on to serve with Teddy Roosevelt and the Rough Riders in the Spanish-American War, and in World Wars I and II. In World War II, three all-African-American units — the 92nd and 93rd infantries and the Tuskegee Airmen — won headlines for their accomplishments as groups. Yet no recognition came for their individual acts of heroism. The African-American units were integrated into U.S. Army forces in 1952.

It seemed unjust to Powell that despite all their service, there was no monument to these brave soldiers. He worked with Representative John Conyers, who introduced a joint resolution declaring July 28, 1992, as Buffalo Soldier Day and calling for construction of the long-sought monument. And in one of his last acts as chairman of the Joint Chiefs of Staff, Powell authorized a study of African-American achievements during World War II to set the record straight.

"I am deeply mindful of the debt I owe to those who went before me," Powell said when the monument to the Buffalo Soldiers was at last unveiled. "I will never forget that the spirit of the Buffalo Soldier will only be satisfied when the day comes that there are no more firsts for blacks to achieve — when we no longer measure progress in America by firsts for anyone, but only by lasts; when that great day comes when all Americans believe and know they are equal."

To Powell, equality means living by universally accepted standards. When he addressed the 1994 graduating class of Howard University, a largely African-American institution in Washington, D.C., the students listened politely but silently. Earlier that year, outside speakers from the Nation of Islam and some of the students had tried to stir up anti-Jewish sentiments. The college's reputation sagged when the media reported that some students cheered the hateful rhetoric.

But Powell told the students to avoid the trap of hatred not for the sake of the victims, but for their own sake. He said it would be a breach of faith in their own history for them to show tolerance for any philosophy based on ethnic or racial hatred.

"There is great wisdom in the message of self-reliance, of education, of hard work, and of the need to raise strong families," Powell told them. "But there is utter foolishness, there is evil, and there is danger in the message of hatred or of condoning violence, however cleverly the message is packaged or entertainingly it is presented. We must find nothing to stand up and cheer about or applaud in a message of racial or ethnic hatred."

Powell has built credibility with all Americans because to him, what is right is transcendent over one or another group's perceived interests. Powell earned praise and honor around the world as a result of the outcome of the Gulf War. President George Bush said Powell "has brought inspiration, strength, and the true spirit of heroism to the world's current struggle for humanity," and embraced Powell in a standing-room-only crowd of African-American veterans. Powell led the victory parade down Chicago's Michigan Avenue, where spectators lined up fifteen rows deep — 300,000 of them — to wave flags and toss confetti.

President Bill Clinton gave Powell the Presidential Medal of Freedom and saluted him with a twenty-one-gun salute and military flyover. Even Queen Elizabeth II of England, because of Powell's contribution during the Gulf War, bestowed on him an honorary knighthood.

Powell — the great warrior for peace — is a hero because as he climbs to the heights he beckons the troops to follow him toward achievement. "I'll never forget that I climbed on the backs of the contributions, sacrifices, and blood of others who will never see the top. But the climb is not over. It will never be over until all Americans believe with the depth of their souls, that they are not limited in any way in this country except by their own willingness to work and their own dreams."

COLIN POWELL'S RULES

Over the years, Colin Powell has collected — and written down on note cards — thirteen rules:

1. It ain't as bad as you think. It will look better in the morning.

2. Get mad. Then get over it.

3. Avoid having your ego so close to your position that, when your position falls, your ego goes with it.

4. It can be done!

5. Be careful what you choose. You may get it.

6. Don't let adverse facts stand in the way of a good decision.

7. You can't make someone else's choices. You shouldn't let someone else make yours.

8. Check small things.

9. Share credit.

10. Remain calm. Be kind.

11. Have a vision. Be demanding.

12. Don't take the counsel of your fears or naysayers.

13. Perpetual optimism is a force multiplier.

John Rollins

John Rollins wondered if the cotton was worth hoeing. Only twelve, but wise beyond his years, he worked beside his mother, Claudia, and his older brother, Wayne, on the family's eighty-acre north Georgia farm. If they were fortunate, they might clear five dollars per bale, along with cotton seed for the cows. It was a pittance even by Depression standards for the work and investment that went into growing mostly cotton, field corn for the livestock, and a smattering of truck crops.

Rollins and his mother milked cows and he peddled the dairy products, along with some of the vegetables, in nearby Chattanooga. Tomatoes and string beans brought a fairly good price, if they could be brought to town early enough in the summer. Whether peddling or farming, it was hard work for the boy, and even harder for his mother. Yet Claudia Rollins and her sons had no choice. Since her husband, the boys' father, had been virtually incapacitated by a stroke, they had to work if they were going to pay their bills and keep food on the table. So Rollins and his brothers learned early about hard work and assuming a grown man's burden.

Looking back, he has no complaints. "When I was growing up, if you slept past 4 A.M., my father felt you would never amount to anything," Rollins recalls. "We went to bed early, had no television or radio. I remember it as a wonderful life."

There were no school buses, and Rollins walked nine miles a day each way to school; in high school, however, the walk was only six miles each way. The easiest path would have been for the Rollins boys to accept their lot and slip into an obscure life of subsistence farming. But Rollins' mother wouldn't allow that to happen. She knew her boys had more to contribute than back-breaking labor the rest of their lives, and she carefully taught them about the meaning of opportunity.

At night, before the boys were tucked in bed, she read to them — not fairy tales, but stories of success. "Mother read us all the Horatio Alger stories at night," John Rollins recounts. "She kept telling us that we could make our lives count. 'I can; I will' was what I came to believe." Given that his beginnings were anything but promising, Rollins' business successes and heroic efforts to show young people how to make something of themselves are testament to the veracity of her advice.

When Rollins graduated from high school in 1934, he tried his hand at farming. But after a year of effort, he had twenty dollars profit to show for it. Then, with a partner, he went into the bedspread business. They bought sheeting and thread and took them to country families to sew into bedspreads, selling the finished products roadside. But the business did poorly and their used car was repossessed.

Next he worked in construction, and then as a ditchdigger. He traveled to Chattanooga for work, where George T. Smith, an older, childless businessman took an interest in him. Smith was superintendent of the Walsch-Weidner Plant, and helped Rollins get a job. "George Smith had an office on Main Street and I would stop in to see him and talk, and he would encourage me. Sometimes he'd give me a ride with him when he went to collect rents on Saturdays. And we would talk."

Smith got Rollins a job in the boiler shop of the plant; he was responsible for keeping the furnaces going and also worked as a boilermaker, machinist, and at other jobs. "I was grinding with an emery wheel and dust was coming down my neck and I thought I had the worst job in the world," Rollins remembers.

During those days of the deep Depression, with scores of men standing in line looking for work, it was the policy of the company to hire five men every morning and at night fire the three who did the least work. "I was strong as an ox with lots of stamina, so I kept my job," Rollins recalls, "but I felt sorry for the older men, many with families, who almost wept when they were let go. They desperately needed the money."

One day at work he came across a newspaper, and a poem on one of the pages caught his eye:

"You may know your economics, your
    philosophy, and such,
But all the knowledge you have gathered
    won't amount to much,
Unless you have the courage of the
    factory or the shop
And can start to climb the ladder from
    the bottom to the top."

Rollins read the poem and told himself he had to have a bright future because at the moment he couldn't go much lower on the ladder. To get out of that trap, he had to move on to better work. But to do that, he realized that he needed more education. He went to school at night and took correspondence courses in mechanical engineering, English literature, grammar, and drafting. "You have to prepare yourself," Rollins said to himself. "You don't have a chance to pitch in the World Series if you can't throw a baseball over the plate."

By 1940 World War II was about to spread to America and Rollins wanted to get a job as a munitions inspector. He applied for a job in Philadelphia twelve times, despite his fear of moving up with the Yankees. His friends in the South advised him to tell jokes on himself, "because those Yankees don't enjoy jokes on them" and to say "Yes, Ma'am" and "No, Ma'am" a lot.

"I guess I worked harder to get that job than any other job before or since," Rollins says. "Every time they said, 'You don't have a college education, you don't have the necessary experience, you don't have this, you don't have the other, we're looking at some other people'."

Finally, on the thirteenth try, he got the job, and on the first day of work he was promoted because he had practical experience. "I was finding out about government and bureaucracy," he says. He was also finding out about the value of tenacity. "I tell young people don't ever give up when you are turned down for a job. Just keep on."

After this experience, Rollins worked for the Crosley Corporation in Cincinnati, leaving a year later to work for Bendix Radio in Baltimore. This time his hard work was recognized, and he was given the opportunity to manage three plants. One day he walked into one of the plants and saw a desk sitting in the middle of the floor. No one knew who ordered it put there. "Get it the hell out of here," Rollins ordered, "or someone will sit down and within two weeks he'll be indispensable." Rollins also worked briefly for a Baltimore aircraft company.

On a vacation, driving his Ford toward the Atlantic shore of Delaware in the Lewes area, Rollins' car began giving him trouble. He pulled into service station after service station, seeking help. But none was to be found. An opportunity, however, was.

Rollins figured other people in that area needed service for their cars as well, and decided to open a Ford dealership. He learned how to sell cars and moved to the coastal area permanently. He started with a partner, a man in his sixties with whom Rollins used to fish. Each of them put up five hundred dollars, and they borrowed ten thousand dollars from a bank. With ten people in the business altogether, they sold Fords in an old building with no air conditioning.

While he was selling Fords and acquiring more dealerships, he was also remembering the times he tried to get a job as a salesman but couldn't, because he didn't own a car. The best person for the job wasn't hired; businesses were hiring the car instead of the person, a practice he thought unfair and unwise. "A salesman should no more have to have his own car than a secretary own a typewriter," he reasoned, a slogan he would later use as a cornerstone of salesmanship.

From his musing came the birth of a new industry. Why not offer to lease cars and trucks to businesses and provide the service and maintenance for them in the bargain? He started doing exactly that in 1951, with the slogan, "Troubles cease when you lease."

As his business flourished, Rollins also expanded his horizons to include politics. In 1952 he was elected the first Republican lieutenant governor of Delaware in twenty years. He served a four-year term, and then turned his attention back to his leasing business to expand into trucks.

Rollins and his associate Henry Tippie began looking for bank loans to expand. After unsuccessfully knocking on many doors, they finally got an interview with a man who listened to their story, and told them he had two problems making a loan to them: "We don't make loans to individuals and we don't make any loans for under a million dollars."

Without batting an eye, Rollins knew what to do: he incorporated and upped his request to a million. His first big deal turned out to be for three hundred cars and two hundred trucks, and he was in business on a vaster scale than he ever thought likely or possible.

"For the first interval of my life I put all my energies into building up my business interests," Rollins describes. He knew that it would take enormous effort to succeed. "I once owned a scrawny racehorse — a mare. She had so much heart, she just kept running. I've seen that quality in horses. I've seen it in men. I don't think you ever have great success unless you have a complete commitment and a fierce desire to win."

It was that intensity he invested in his own run for governor of the State of Delaware in 1960. He spoke at dinners, he knocked on doors, he passed out pamphlets until he was exhausted. But it still wasn't enough to overcome his minority party status, and he was narrowly defeated.

"It was the best thing that ever happened to me," Rollins later remarked. "In fact, I have always felt that things often happen for the best." Rollins believes that even defeats and failures have a special value, no matter how unpleasant. "Failures teach you something. Sometimes I'd like not to have been taught so much." Among the things Rollins learned was that his energies could be better spent in business, and in helping others. He stayed interested in politics, and over the years was an advisor to several presidents.

To regain his strength after the loss, he traveled to the island of Jamaica. There, Caribbean breezes soothed him, days in the sun restored him, and great fishing adventures revitalized him. But most of all, he was touched by the kindness, generosity, and industriousness of the Jamaican people. He recognized that what many of them sought was the opportunity to provide for themselves and their families, and decided to establish a number of businesses to create jobs and in other ways demonstrate his commitment to the Jamaican people, and especially to their children.

"I wanted to provide about ten thousand jobs for those wonderful people," he says. Over the years, he has: funded the multi-million-dollar restoration of the Rose Hall Great House, a plantation built in the early 1700s; built eleven hundred hotel rooms and The Palms, a group of condominiums; restored a local landmark, the Mount Zion Church; and given land to the S.O.S. Village, a nonprofit orphanage for one hundred children. In addition, he has established a scholarship fund for Jamaican students at Reinhardt College in Georgia. Rollins' wife (his third), lawyer Michele Metrinko, is president of Rollins Jamaica Ltd. and a counselor in all of his undertakings — as well as the mother of the four youngest of his ten children.

By the late 1960s Rollins had acquired seventeen companies, including the much larger — its customer base included three out of four of the Fortune 500 companies — Matlack Trucking Company. Among the properties were a number of chemical waste businesses, which became Rollins Environmental Services. (John Rollins, Jr., one of four children of his first marriage, directs with him the companies that bear his name. Jeffrey Rollins, one of two sons born during his second marriage, plays a key role in Rollins Environmental Services.)

Because dealing with hazardous wastes was such a hot environmental issue, Rollins had more than his share of problems running the company. "I think when Rollins Environmental got in trouble, watching over it and turning it around and bringing it back to success gave me a lot of satisfaction. Turning around a big reverse is hard. Looking back, it was fun, too."

Rollins also worked with his brother to build an electronic communications empire.

Together, they owned radio, cable, and television stations in Virginia, California, Delaware, New York, West Virginia, and Florida, until they sold them.

Altogether, John Rollins personally, or in conjunction with his brother, founded six companies traded on New York stock exchanges, employed tens of thousands of people and generated more than a billion dollars of revenue every year.

One particular bit of wisdom that has guided Rollins is that it is no fool who gives what he cannot keep to gain what he cannot lose. Keeping this in mind when his success in business put him in a position to help others, Rollins set a heroic example for many.

It is remarkable that Rollins has accomplished so much by giving chances to people many others would not. One of the first people he ever hired was a man he met in a bar — Rollins never checked his references. The man worked out well and Rollins has since made it a point to hire members of Alcoholics Anonymous.

"I went to so many AA meetings to speak, some thought I was an alcoholic, but I wasn't. I just wanted to give a chance to some smart people who wanted to start over again. I like to help," Rollins explains.

Yet it isn't only idealism that motivates him:

"We have a great belief that if you treat other people well, they'll work mighty hard for you," he says. So, he looks for people who are likely to appreciate being given a chance.

"I've told my search committees to look for the ethnics whose mothers and fathers were immigrants to this country. They love this country with a new, fierce, and wonderful love. They'll starve to educate their children. And it's very apparent in the work ethics of this second generation of ethnics.

"Nothing is more rewarding than to help people develop to their full potential. It is amazing how they develop when you take a special interest in them. After all, to achieve success, one needs the people around. I promote personal incentives in business. I love to see our associates making money because then I know I am, too."

Because Horatio Alger stories did so much to inspire him when he was young, Rollins has been a member of the Horatio Alger Association of Distinguished Americans for more than thirty years, and is the chairman emeritus of its board of directors. (Coincidentally, through the Horatio Alger Association, Rollins became involved with a son of Jamaican immigrants and another American hero, General Colin Powell.)

Through the society, he speaks to groups

of young people to pass along his enthusiasm for the American system, through which a poor farm boy from Georgia with only a high school education can achieve monumental success. "It's my opinion that the best way to help anyone is to give them the opportunity to do something for themselves. That's why it is so imperative that business leaders today pay attention to the education of our youth," he says.

His excitement about the opportunities available to young people is contagious: "There are wonderful opportunities, given our fast-moving technology," he tells them. And then, he looks for his own opportunities . . . to give them scholarships. He funds dozens of them a year, including many for students in the rural communities of Delaware, his adopted state. In fact, he has even been known to award scholarships to students who compete for them, but lose, as he did in 1994 when presenting a five-thousand-dollar scholarship to the finalist of a high school's Horatio Alger Association contest. After naming the winner, Rollins felt the other two finalists were so deserving he gave each of them a scholarship as well — out of his own pocket.

"I was particularly sympathetic because I had many of the same hardships these girls have had," he said. The main difference, he observed, is that their grades were better.

"One big secret of success is a deep-down desire. Whether people or race-horses, they have to have a fierce desire to win."

"That little bit extra is the key to success."

"Don't procrastinate. Tomorrow is not today's best labor-saving device."

"I've been successful and on the verge of being broke, and successful is a hell of a lot nicer. Still, you've got to have the steel and drive to take risks."

"The important thing in business is to make a decision. You can go broke exercising patience. Make the decision with your best judgment and then make it work."

"Family is the most important thing in the world."

"The most valuable asset you have is your character and your integrity."

"You have to realize that your building stones and your foundation are your integrity. Unless you tell the truth and people can depend on you, you can't become very successful. People have to have faith in you."

Jonas Edward Salk

It was the summer of 1952, and Dr. Jonas Salk faced a critical decision. It had been the worst year of the worst polio epidemic in history, with nearly sixty thousand new cases reported. Salk was convinced that the polio vaccine he'd developed was safe and effective. But how certain was he? Was his confidence in it sufficient to risk injecting it into his wife and three sons? Absolutely. "I wasn't going to inoculate anybody else without first inoculating myself and my own children," he says. "The responsibility I felt for giving the vaccine to others was greater than the responsibility I felt for inoculating my own family."

Trying the vaccine on his family didn't seem like much of a risk to Salk. His research and experiments had proved to him that his theories were correct. Salk had discovered that a killed virus produces antibodies as does a live virus. A vaccine made of polio virus killed with formaldehyde, he concluded, could prompt the human body to produce antibodies to polio, just the way the live virus could. People could be protected from polio without being infected with the disease.

It was on a warm day at the end of June when Salk went to the D. T. Watson Home for Crippled Children near Pittsburgh to give the first young volunteers — children who had already been infected with one of the three strains of polio — their first injection of the clear pink liquid that he'd formulated. Despite his dislike of causing them pain by giving them injections, Salk vaccinated each child himself. Salk "obviously was not just a scientist on an experiment but a man deeply concerned about the human importance of an experiment," observed Lucile Cochran, a nurse and administrator at the Watson home.

He came back to the Watson home that evening to check on the children, to make sure none had become ill. "When you inoculate children with a polio vaccine, you don't sleep well for a number of months," Salk said at the time. He came back to the home so often to check on the children that most staff members became familiar with his kind smile; when he was due for a visit, the cook would bake his favorite strawberry pie.

Salk couldn't be sure whether the vaccinated children would be protected from infection by live polio virus; the only way to find out would be to infect the children with polio. But the children produced so many antibodies within six weeks of injection that he was confident the vaccine worked.

One set of test results was especially encouraging. To blood drawn from the inoculated children, Salk mixed in live polio virus. The virus killed blood cells produced before the vaccination, but those produced afterward thrived. Apparently, the antibodies were working.

The testing process proceeded with no publicity — few outside the Watson home, especially the press, knew of it. "I never thought it possible that so many people could keep a secret so well," Salk later said. But in time, word got out. Newspaper reporters learned that some "good news" was forthcoming about a vaccine, and *Time* magazine predicted that if field trials were successful, a vaccine against polio could be available the next year.

The eagerness with which the public waited for such news was understandable. Every year in the summer and early fall, thousands of children would contract polio, which is transmitted through the mouth and nose, forcing the closure of public swimming pools. Although it most commonly affected children, which is why it was known as infantile paralysis, adults could become infected as well. Franklin Delano Roosevelt, for example, was stricken at thirty-nine, conducting his entire presidency from a wheelchair as a result.

And, previous experimental vaccines against polio had met with disastrous results: some children became paralyzed from them. In much of the medical community, polio was seen as a unique phenomenon to which conventional means of attack did not apply. News of yet another vaccine attempt met with considerable derision. Why would Salk's be more effective than its predecessors?

Salk was born in 1914 into the Jewish family of Daniel and Dora Salk. The family (Salk has two younger brothers) moved from upper Manhattan to the Bronx, where Salk distinguished himself as a student. He went to a high school for exceptional students, read everything he could get his hands on, and was a perfectionist about his schoolwork. He graduated from New York University School of Medicine in 1939, and completed his internship three years later.

In 1942, he began a National Research Council Fellowship at the University of Michigan to work on a vaccine against another widespread disease: influenza. At the time, influenza was far more of a scourge than it is today; in 1918 for example, the disease killed 850,000 Americans, including 44,000 soldiers.

Through his research with Dr. Thomas Francis, Jr., Salk learned that killed viruses stimulated the development of antibody levels as much as the live virus did itself. Their discovery led to development of a vaccine against influenza, which protected American troops during World War II and is still in use today.

Salk began his own research at the University of Pittsburgh Medical School in 1947. Working under a grant, he assembled a team of researchers and developed a laboratory that was to classify strains of polio viruses.

When the poliomyelitis virus enters the body, it moves to the intestinal tract and eventually travels to the central nervous system. There, it may kill or temporarily injure nerve cells that control muscles, causing paralysis. Sometimes a small group of muscles is affected, sometimes the paralysis is widespread. The legs are affected more often than the arms, but polio may partially or completely paralyze a single limb. Thousands of Americans today have a withered arm or leg as a result of a polio infection decades ago.

When the virus reaches the spinal cord and/or brain stem, it can paralyze muscles that control breathing, swallowing, and other reflexive functions, ultimately causing death. Children with the most severe cases, who could no longer breathe without mechanical help, were treated with an iron lung. Pulling out a diaphragm at one end of the machine created a vacuum inside that caused the child to inhale. Pushing in the diaphragm caused the child to exhale. These children needed care for the rest of their lives. The image of a child in an iron lung was made frighteningly familiar during fund-raising campaigns by the National Foundation for Infantile Paralysis, which later became the March of Dimes Birth Defects Foundation.

But among the crowds of enthusiastic parents awaiting news of a vaccine, were scientific critics. One of the harshest was Dr. Albert Sabin, who had been working on his own vaccine — one comprised of a weak strain of live polio virus — since 1946. Sabin believed that additional, extensive tests were necessary before a vaccine like Salk's could be considered safe. He wanted to vaccinate children who had never had polio, and then test them again some time later to see how well they had produced antibodies. He had said a killed virus was impractical and wouldn't produce results that would last long enough.

"Dr. Salk is a very cautious man," said Dr. Thomas Rivers during the heated debate about how to proceed with the vaccine and at what pace. "Some people want to go faster than he wants to go. Some want to throw all he has got out of the window and try something else. . . ." But Rivers, like most Americans, wanted to get on with saving lives. "Have we the right to wait until the ideal vaccine comes along? Should we go ahead and use this vaccine that seems to be effective right now when people are crying for it?," he asked.

Salk announced the success of the vaccine at a March 1953 press conference that coincided with the publication of the results. Parents, desperate to protect their children from polio, eagerly participated in vaccine field trials; eventually, 1,839,000 children, Salk's three sons among them, took part in the trials. Many proudly wore "Polio Pioneer" buttons.

By the spring of 1955, the field trial results were in. The announcement was made at the University of Michigan, and Salk brought his wife and three sons to share in the triumph. Radio and television stations were poised to broadcast the results to an eager public worldwide. When the report was handed out in the pressroom, otherwise dour newsmen shouted with excitement. "The vaccine works!," the report concluded. "It is safe, effective, and potent."

In 1955, when massive inoculation programs got underway, the tragic picture of a child in an iron lung was pushed off the news pages by a new photograph, one portraying

American children and their parents standing in lines that extended for blocks and blocks at every clinic and school where children could be vaccinated.

Thanks to Salk and his team of researchers, the fear was taken out of summer and swimming pools and drinking fountains. Millions of arms and legs were kept straight and countless lives prevented from ending too soon. The Salk vaccine effectively ended polio as a threat to health in the United States. And Salk received not a cent for any of it. When Edward R. Murrow asked him about patenting the vaccine, Salk replied that the vaccine "belongs to the people. Could you patent the sun?"

The modest Salk objected that the product of his team effort became known as the Salk vaccine, but there was little he could do to change it now that the country had found a true medical hero. He refused a New York City ticker-tape parade up Broadway, and turned down a chance to have Marlon Brando star in his life story. He also passed up the opportunity to endorse a line of pajamas that read, "Thank you, Dr. Salk." He did, however, accept a citation from President Dwight Eisenhower and a Congressional Gold Medal for "great achievement in the field of medicine."

In 1961, the Salk vaccine was largely replaced by another vaccine: Sabin's. The biggest advantage of the Sabin vaccine over the Salk vaccine was that a few drops of it could be placed on a sugar cube and given orally instead of by injection. Therefore it could be administered by anyone, instead of only by trained medical professionals, and meant fewer injections for children. Most of the polio inoculations given today are from the Sabin rather than the Salk vaccine.

Thanks to Salk's innovative research half a century ago, polio is now on the verge of becoming another footnote, like smallpox, in the history of disease. Thanks to Rotary International and the World Health Organization, which distribute polio vaccine internationally, polio is expected to be completely eradicated worldwide by the year 2000.

Rotary International began the process in the late 1970s, when the Philippines asked the business organization to fund polio vaccinations there. Immediately after treatments began, the disease declined and within a few years was practically eliminated. Soon, other countries asked for help as well, and the million-plus member, worldwide service organization eventually raised $245 million for the project.

The results were dramatic and swift. Polio was virtually eliminated in Latin America after only five years. Hundreds of millions of children are being inoculated in China now that Rotary paid five million dollars to build a vaccine production plant there. After less than ten years of the Rotary program, almost six hundred million children have been inoculated. In addition to providing polio vaccine, the Rotary program, whenever possible, also inoculates children against diphtheria, tetanus, pertussis, measles, and tuberculosis.

To continue the struggle against disease, Salk formed the Salk Institute, which provides scientists from around the world with the opportunity to carry out fundamental research in the fields of biology related to human disease such as: cancer, genetics, birth defects, brain function, and immunologic disorders.

At the age of seventy-five, Salk began work on yet another vaccine to combat the new scourge of the world — AIDS. After conquering one health menace, can he defeat yet another? Though he is now in his eighties, he continues to try. Once again, he has employed a killed-virus technology, and once again scoffers have denigrated his efforts. Thus far, the result of his research is an immunogen to be administered to the already infected to slow or prevent the onset of disease; he is also working on a vaccine that would prevent infection. A "vaccine" of sorts, the immunogen was to become the first AIDS-inhibiting product to undergo large-scale tests in America. If it works, he will have contributed to the control of three major diseases in his lifetime.

Although Salk wanted no money for his polio vaccine, no profit of any kind for his gift to humanity, like it or not he has the gratitude of mankind. "He has the reputation among some scientists as a god," one AIDS researcher has commented. Generations of children around the world, their arms and legs straight, their health protected from a disease that no longer exists, have a doctor to thank — an American hero named Jonas Salk.

AS JONAS SALK SEES THINGS

"Many wise individuals have had no formal education. . . . They possess a powerful intuitive faculty and are able to learn from experience, from what they observe."

"Belief, knowledge, and truth must not be confused — each must be used appropriately."

"The wise will . . . tend to give in the short term, to obtain gain in the long term. The unwise tend to take now but will likely lose later."

"Is not wisdom a basis for selection among men, and is it not the ideal toward which some men have always aspired?"

"Even though Death eventually wins over Life so far as the individual is concerned, Life wins over Death in the perpetuation of the species."

Dave Thomas

Dave Thomas stood in the Missing Persons
Office of the Philadelphia Police Department full of hope, anticipation, and dread.
He was twenty-one years old, fresh out of
the U.S. Army, and determined to find his
birth mother, Mollie. It had been eight years
since he'd learned that he had been adopted
when he was six weeks old, and all the
questions he'd asked himself in that time
raced through his mind: Why did his parents
give him up? What were they doing now?
Had they had any other children? Did he
have brothers or sisters?

Using letters Thomas's birth mother had
sent to his adoptive grandmother, the police
were able to find an address in nearby Cam-
den, New Jersey. There, Thomas met his birth
grandparents: his grandfather was a tailor; his
grandmother was very ill. And he began to
learn about his past.

Although his birth mother had lived near
Philadelphia, Thomas, who would later go on

to establish the vastly successful Wendy's chain of hamburger restaurants, was born at a home for unwed mothers in Atlantic City. His birth father, Sam, a stockbroker who had died years before, may never have known he'd conceived a child with Mollie. Married at thirty-five, Sam and his wife had had a son, Thomas's half brother, who became a college professor.

Some time after giving up Thomas for adoption, his birth mother married a man named Joe, but she never had any more children. She worked in a restaurant as a waitress, and died of rheumatic fever. Ironically, his adoptive mother, Auleva, died of the same disease two years later. Thomas's adoptive father had a hard time keeping a job, so the boy's early life was filled with disruption and often being uprooted.

One constant in Thomas's youth was his adoptive maternal grandmother, Minnie Sinclair, with whom he spent several summers after his mother died. Herself widowed when her husband was killed in a railroad accident, Sinclair had raised her own four children alone. Thomas describes her as the strongest influence in his life when he was young; she was the one who told him he was adopted.

"I had a lot of respect for her. She had so little, but she made so much out of it. . . .

She believed if you worked hard, you made things happen," he wrote in his autobiography, *Dave's Way*.

"Hard work is good for the soul," his grandmother used to tell him, "and it keeps you from feeling sorry for yourself because you don't have time." Hard work has been the power behind Thomas's success — hard work and motivation.

Thomas began working at the age of twelve, passing himself off as fifteen to get a job in a Knoxville, Tennessee, grocery store. Thomas lost that job, as well as the next one he got, working at the counter at Walgreen's. His adoptive father didn't think much of Thomas's achievements in business. "You'll never keep a job! I'll be supporting you for the rest of your life!," he told him one day.

That thought motivated Thomas to succeed at his future jobs. He soon started working at the Regas Restaurant in downtown Knoxville — one of the city's finest. "I became used to putting out a lot of volume when I was very young; I just thought that it was the way you were supposed to do it. If somebody pays you, it was up to you to perform."

The family then moved to Fort Wayne, Indiana where Thomas got another restaurant job. When his adoptive father decided to move the family again, fifteen-year-old Thomas decided to stay. He lived at the YMCA, worked fifty hours a week at the restaurant, and continued to attend Fort Wayne Central High. He quit high school just after the tenth grade and soon found himself very lonely. He moved in with relatives of the restaurant owner, where he experienced caring, supportive family life for the first time; he'd never forget it. Nor would he forget Lorraine Buskirk, with whom he worked at a Fort Wayne restaurant — she's been his wife since 1954 and is the mother of their five children.

In 1950, at the age of seventeen, Thomas joined the U.S. Army. He made it a practice to volunteer for work, and when there was a staff sergeant position to fill, someone remembered. "A little initiative will improve your luck nine days out of ten," he maintains.

Soon after being discharged from the army, Thomas met the man who would become his first professional role model. When he was twenty-five years old and learning about restaurant management, "I wanted to be like Kenny King," Thomas recalls. King owned about twenty restaurants — mostly drive-ins — in Cleveland, Ohio; in the late 1950s, he was making $100,000 a year. Thomas still remembers the Cadillac that King drove, and he also took note of King's expensive clothes, his suite of offices, and their costly furniture.

At a meeting, King told him without apology: "Hey, son, this is America. If I can do it so can you. All you've got to do is work hard and have ethics. In the morning you've got to get up and look at the guy in the mirror. You've got to be honest with the guy in the mirror before anyone else." In addition, King offered other advice: "The support of your family is the most important thing that you have in your life." And, King told him, "I've got the money, I've got the responsibility to share it."

With King in mind, Thomas took a big gamble and went out on his own. "When the time is right to make a move, a person just knows it," he says. In January of 1962, he moved to Columbus, Ohio, to take over some struggling Kentucky Fried Chicken restaurants a friend of his had bought.

His first step was to get rid of the unproductive employees. He cleaned up the restaurants, and improved employee morale and customer confidence. He pared down the menu, focusing the business entirely on chicken, identified the business with a sign depicting buckets of chicken, and then advertised and promoted as much as he could. And every day he kept track of the most important indicators of success or failure.

By virtue of luck coupled with his own genius, Thomas had ventured into his first big restaurant success. He and his partner were able to sell the restaurants to the parent company, making Dave Thomas a millionaire by the time he was thirty-five. He now had the seed money to open the chain of hamburger restaurants he had dreamed about owning since his childhood.

Wendy's Old Fashioned Hamburgers, which is named for one of Thomas's daughters, was launched in 1969. The chain featured upscale hamburgers, a concept that worked well in both high- and low-income areas. Thomas began franchising Wendy's restaurants in 1973, and as of this writing, there are more than forty-five hundred Wendy's in thirty-four countries. Annual sales have grown to more than $4.2 billion and the chain employs about 130,000 people. The "Where's the Beef?" advertising campaign was one of the most successful in marketing history, and even became a presidential election campaign slogan.

Believing in hard work earned Thomas his military promotion. Taking the initiative made it possible for him to find his birth parents. Finding an appropriate role model enabled him to realize his professional goal. How he has put into practice King's advice about family and sharing the wealth is what wins him his status as an American hero.

"Families are the most important thing," he has written. "You have to have a job to support your family and you have to have religion to keep family, job, and philosophy together. And then you have an obligation to help people who need help."

The group of people for which Thomas has become champion is children in need of adoptive families. "It may seem strange that I should support adoption, because my adopted childhood was not all that happy. But that's not the way I look at it. . . . Had I not been adopted, I could have ended up as a ward of the state or raised in a county orphanage. So the way I see it, adoption turned out to be a big plus for me," he wrote.

He supports adoption because he believes too many children are growing up in makeshift facilities. "Without a home and affection, the chances for making it in this world are mighty slim," he believes. He also feels that children raised without homes often wind up causing trouble for the rest of society. Families, if you ask Dave Thomas, are the basis on which the world works.

As a result, he appears in radio and television public service announcements urging families to adopt. He grants hundreds of interviews per year as part of his campaign to raise awareness that there are thousands of children awaiting adoption, and to educate prospective parents about the adoption process.

However, Thomas does more than talk about adoption. Because of the strength of his opinions, President George Bush asked him in 1990 to become national spokesman for the Presidential Initiative on Adoption called "Adoption Works . . . For Everyone." The goal of the program was to encourage adoption of 100,000 children per year, many of whom are older, emotionally or physically challenged, or part of sibling groups wishing to remain together — in other words, children with special needs.

And Thomas puts his money where his mouth is, too. Wendy's offers adoption benefits, just like maternity benefits, to its employees. The package provides financial assistance and paid leave time for employees who adopt. An employee receives up to four thousand dollars in fees and legal costs if he or she adopts a child, and six thousand dollars if the family adopts a child with special needs.

"We help cover the costs of the adoption process, including the individual and family counseling sometimes needed to help children make a smoother adjustment into their new families," Thomas explains. In its first four years, the company spent about sixty-five thousand dollars for nineteen adoptions compared to five million dollars for maternity claims. "It's not expensive to do," Thomas said. "Profit is not a dirty word with any of us but we have to give something back. That's where responsibility comes in."

The program worked so well for Wendy's that Thomas was motivated to write to the heads of the Fortune 1000 companies, America's largest, urging them to offer adoption benefits as well. In addition, he travels all over the country urging other executives to grant adoption benefits to their employees. "I hope someday that every organization — private and public — will provide adoption benefits to give people incentive to adopt," he says.

To promote adoption Thomas has also created the Dave Thomas Foundation, which is funded in part by the profits of his two books, *Dave's Way* and *Well Done*. *Dave's Way*, his plainspoken autobiography, has sold more than 350,000 copies. *Well Done* is an inspirational book about achieving success the honest way. The foundation has already produced half a million copies of "A Beginner's Guide to Adoption," a thirteen-page booklet written with the assistance of adoption experts and distributed to adoption agencies across the country as well as to individuals interested in learning more about how to adopt a child. (For a copy, send a note or card with your name, address, and ZIP code to: Free Adoption Guide, The Dave Thomas Foundation for Adoption, P.O. Box 7164, Dublin, OH 43017.)

Thomas also makes it a point to support other children's charities, such as St. Jude's Research Hospital in Memphis, the Ohio State University Cancer Research Institute, and Recreation Unlimited, which offers camping and recreation opportunities to disabled children. He is a member of the board of the Foundation of the Children's Home Society of Florida, a child advocacy group. He and his wife have contributed more than half a million dollars to this organization and have helped establish a twenty-four-hour kids crisis hotline and emergency home for young victims of abuse and neglect in Fort Lauderdale.

He is also a generous contributor to education. "Look for ways to support education," he recommends. "Education gives a person the opportunity for a better life, and every person is entitled to that." And, although he didn't need to, he proved it by earning his GED from Coconut Creek High School in Fort Lauderdale in 1993, forty-five years after dropping out of high school; his class elected him "Most Likely to Succeed." Dropping out "was a big mistake," he reflects. "I should never have done it. There's no way in today's world that I could have done what I did without a better education." His donations to Duke University in Durham, North Carolina, have been so substantial that the university built the R. David Thomas Center for executive education, where business leaders who are not enrolled in MBA programs can study.

Thomas has also been recognized by the Horatio Alger Association — his award was presented by Norman Vincent Peale — and became its president. Participating in the association has provided Thomas with an avenue through which he could emphasize another factor he believes is essential in any equation for success: role models. Under the association's aegis, Thomas launched a program to bring members together with high school students from around the country. The program now helps thousands of young people by giving them role models and examples to follow, and by helping them formulate their own goals.

"Everybody has a need for heroes . . . ," says Thomas, "people to mold themselves after, people they want to be like. You have to be able to dream, but those dreams should be about real people who have actually done things. . . . People need role models — I think — at every stage of their life . . . not just when they're kids."

And, Thomas says, don't expect a role model to come along all by him or herself. "There are plenty of classy people out there who want to help. Instead of waiting for somebody to take you under their wing, go out there and find a good wing to climb under."

On the other hand, Thomas urges caution about choosing an appropriate role model. "Many people want to link up with superstars. The way I see it, sometimes you can learn more from a common, everyday person who cares about others and who has achieved something than from some guy with a big ego who just wants a bunch of followers.

"Don't just study people who succeed, study people who handle success well. See how people who have succeeded financially live their lives, and learn from that. Some people can't handle money or success. It destroys them. They overbuy, drink, take drugs, become playboys or country clubbers. Eventually they let their businesses slide, too, because they let their egos get in the way of their judgment. They forget about their families, their self-respect, and their fellow human beings."

It's not an easy scenario in which to imagine Dave Thomas. His basic values — the importance he places on a strong family, hard work, and contributing to society — will keep him securely among American heroes.

DAVE THOMAS'S THOUGHTS

"My recipe for success is hard work, patience, honesty, and total commitment."

"Find out how someone became successful, learn from that, and then go out and do it."

"There are never any guarantees, but there are also no rewards without risks."

"Many company founders go down the drain being greedy. If you want to build your company, you have to deal your key people in. But don't give your rights away, either."

"Spread your giving around. I think you need to help everybody a little bit, but not stick with one thing too much."

"Support people who make things happen. Give to charities that really put the bucks to work."

"Give first priority to local causes. Not only will you be able to see the impact, you have the best chance of having a voice in the way the dollars are used."

Elie Wiesel

Elie Wiesel stepped out into the brisk Oslo evening. Night comes early in Norway in December, but tonight the darkness was filled with light. Wiesel, author, teacher, playwright, journalist, lecturer, had just received the Nobel Peace Prize, and thousands of people, flaming torches in hand, waited to congratulate him. They sang the international anthem of peaceful resistance to evil, "We Shall Overcome," repeating the verse, "We shall live in peace" over and over.

This torchlight parade in 1986 was a far cry from those that traumatized Wiesel's life half a century earlier. Then, Nazi youth that paraded through the streets of Germany with torches sang hymns of hatred. Their songs eventually led to Wiesel's incarceration in a concentration camp, and the murder of his parents and younger sister. That Elie Wiesel has made the journey from witnessing parades of hatred and destruction to being the honored recipient of a parade recognizing his efforts to combat hatred itself is the embodiment of heroism.

Eliezer Wiesel's long journey began in 1928, when Shlomo and Sarah Wiesel had their second child. He was born in Sighet, a small, but thriving Jewish community in the Hungarian-speaking but Rumanian province of Transylvania. The whole of the community revolved about the family and, through it, the perpetuation of Jewish tradition. Their's was a quiet life, a seemingly harmless life, but one that nonetheless attracted the attention of people hundreds of miles away — people determined to put an end to it.

"The Nazis were clever," Wiesel recalls. "They didn't reveal their plans right away. In the beginning, it was simply a few decrees: a pogrom here and there, and every now and then a few people were arrested. Then there were more arrests, and then some were killed. Then the yellow stars, and then the ghettos, and then the deportations. Again, it was done according to a psychological plan to fool and blind the victim. We really didn't know what they had in store for us."

But young Wiesel found out soon enough, when he and his family were sent to Auschwitz. When the war turned against the Germans, his community was given a day's notice to prepare for deportation by train. The fifteen-year-old boy had watched as his teachers, his rabbis, his neighbors had marched off to the train station. When it was his family's turn to leave behind all that was familiar, he noticed that his gentile neighbors were silent — a silence he came to interpret as evil.

For much of that long train ride the Wiesels believed they were being sent to Hungary to work in a brick factory. But soon all illusions of their fate were stripped away. Wiesel and his father watched as his mother and eight-year-old sister walked off into eternity at Auschwitz. He stayed by his father's side during the year they worked as slave laborers at Buchenwald.

Wiesel asked his father if what they were experiencing was a nightmare from which they would wake up. But the nightmare continued; some months later, he felt the heartbreaking sorrow of helplessly listening to his father's moans as he lay dying in his barracks of hunger and disease. That's when Elie Wiesel took deep within himself the anguish that continues to torment Holocaust survivors long after their persecutors are gone.

When the Germans at last fled the advancing allies, Wiesel stared into a mirror for the first time in a year "and saw a corpse staring back." When the Americans liberated Buchenwald, to which Wiesel had been moved in 1945, Wiesel was one of hundreds of young people with no family and no home to return to. He was impressed with the kindness and caring of the Americans who freed the camps, shared their food with the children, and nursed them back to health. He had never before experienced such generous treatment from gentiles, and he never forgot it.

After the liberation, he was brought to France, a sixteen-year-old numb from suffering and with no concept of a future. There, as if by a miracle, he learned that his two older sisters, Bea and Hilda, were alive. Their reunion was sweet, but since his sisters were struggling to survive just as he was, they were in no position to help him. In France he also found a sense of purpose in his life: he knew he had to testify about the crimes he had witnessed, but he vowed to wait ten years, until he had mastered French sufficiently to communicate the horrors.

"Whoever lives through a trial or takes part in an event that weighs on man's destiny or frees him, is dutybound to transmit what he has seen," Wiesel has said. Not to "transform it into link and promise is to turn it into a gift to death."

From the time he had arrived in France, Wiesel had subsisted on a stipend from a Jewish children's aid group, Oeuvres de Secour aux Enfants. In 1948, he enrolled at the Sorbonne to learn philosophy, but also to survive. As a student, he tutored Jewish children in Bible and Talmud studies. Without the work, he would have been condemned to a life on charity.

He wanted to go to Israel to fight to defend the new country, but was told he was too weak. After various jobs teaching, he became a journalist — he learned one needs no college degree to become a foreign correspondent. He found *Yediot Aharonot*, a newspaper in Israel, that needed news from Paris. He also found that journalism was an excellent way to appease his restlessness and travel the world.

While working as a journalist in France, Wiesel had the opportunity to interview François Mauriac, a noted French literary figure, member of the French Academy, winner of the 1952 Nobel Prize in Literature, and resistance fighter. Mauriac urged him to tell his own story. When Wiesel's self-imposed decade of silence had ended, he wrote an eight-hundred-page memoir in Yiddish entitled *And The World Was Silent*. Although the book is now considered a classic, at the time it was difficult to find a publisher. Even Mauriac's personal intercession could not get it into print. An Argentinean Yiddish publisher printed it in 1956; a shortened version, rewritten in French under the title of *Night* appeared in France in 1960 and was well received.

But it was such a sad book that American publishers at first felt no one would want to read it. Arthur Wang of Hill & Wang eventually bought the book for one hundred dollars; its American paperback version is 128 pages long. In the next two years, Wiesel wrote *Dawn* and *The Accident* for Wang. His contributions to literature began to receive recognition after his publication of *The Town Beyond the Wall* in 1964, when he was awarded the Prix Rivarol in France and two National Jewish Book Council awards in America. To date he has written more than thirty-seven books, and his works are in demand from publishers all over the world.

In the 1950s, Wiesel was to bring his profession to New York, where he wrote for newspapers in Hebrew, Yiddish, and French. He fell in love with New York's energy and optimism, and remembered the kindness with which he had been treated by his American liberators. He decided that if his mission in life were to testify to what had happened during the war, he should do it where the most people could hear his message and where he could do the most good. Toward that end, he became an American citizen in 1963. Although he was criticized for choosing to become an American instead of an Israeli, he hoped that the good he would do in the United States might someday change his critics' minds.

Having heard of the suffering of the Jews in the Soviet Union, in 1965 he traveled there to see it for himself. He saw repression, as he expected, but also observed a defiant spirit that he recorded in his 1966 book, *The Jews of Silence*. His message from that land of suffering was: "Cry out, cry out until you have no more strength to cry. You must enlist public opinion, you must turn to those with influence, you must involve the governments — the hour is late." Wiesel's accounts of the plight of Soviet Jews helped launch the outcry that eventually freed them and others in that restrictive country as well.

His next career step brought him to Boston University where he is a University Professor, teaching philosophy and religious studies, as well as holder of the Andrew Mellon chair in the humanities. As a professor, Wiesel is noted for never teaching the same course twice, choosing to range in topics from author Franz Kafka, to hope and despair in ancient and modern literature, and to the deaths of great masters. Teacher's assistants grade students' papers because Wiesel says he could not bear to cause a student the pain of receiving a bad grade.

Wiesel's restless energy prompts him to travel regularly and frequently for a number of causes, and he supports many institutions around the world. Understandably, he has been active in perpetuating awareness of the Holocaust. In fact, he was the first to use that term, which comes from the Greek for "a sacrifice burnt in its entirety," to describe the destruction of European Jewry. He was chairman of the President's Commission on the Holocaust in 1979, and honorary chairman of the World Gathering of Jewish Holocaust Survivors, at which almost seven thousand survivors gathered in Jerusalem in 1981. After he won the Nobel Peace Prize, one publication ranked him with the pope and the secretary general of the United Nations as one of three who fight for world peace.

One of Wiesel's greatest achievements has been to bridge the distinctions among religions and capture the attention and the conscience of people of all faiths. In fact, a Catholic magazine, *America*, published a special issue in tribute to Wiesel. "Anti-semitic church teachings probably contributed to the catastrophe," Wiesel has noted. "But at the same time, there were Christians who, because of their Christianity, risked their lives and their families' lives to save Jews."

Wiesel has been critical of past popes for their indifference toward Jewish suffering during the war, observing that Adolph Hitler was never excommunicated. He also chastised a contemporary pope for refusing to recognize Israel while receiving her enemies. And yet, Cardinal Jean-Marie Lustiger, archbishop of Paris, said Wiesel "is one of the great theologians of our century." In one of the many ironies of Wiesel's life, this Catholic cleric, who himself had been born Jewish, labors with Wiesel to find the meaning in his suffering.

The archbishop wrote in 1988: "Wiesel has remained a man of faith, even when all evidence of God's presence was destroyed. His testimony — all his work — brings us back not to the horror of the past, but to the threshold where our personal responsibility still operates. He warns us about the nature of the danger that can always surface again. This is Elie Wiesel's mission and what makes his message unique."

Questioning God, challenging God, and yet stubbornly believing in God are recurrent themes in many of Wiesel's works to such an extent that some have called him the Job of Auschwitz. Job, the figure in the Bible best known for keeping his faith despite great tribulation, said of his faith in God after losing family and all possessions: "Though He slay me, yet will I hope in Him."

"I often think of Job and his three friends," says Wiesel. "The three friends tried to find reasons for his suffering. Job didn't want that. He wanted something else, consolation, comforting. He wanted friendship. They gave him an explanation."

This is Wiesel's approach to the Holocaust as well as all other human suffering. What is called for is comfort, not explanations. And, Wiesel has said, explanations about the Holocaust should be left to those who experienced it and no one else, just as the only ones who should feel guilty about it are those who perpetrated it and no one else. He has raised his voice concerning outrages in Cambodia and wherever human conscience must be roused.

Characteristically, Wiesel continually manages to turn his recognitions into opportunities to do even more. Half a century after he was liberated from Auschwitz, he had the chance to exercise the power of his spirit of conciliation through an event concerning the camp itself. During preparations for 1995 ceremonies commemorating the liberation, there had been discord between Jewish groups and Polish president Lech Walesa. Walesa, in his speeches, had not mentioned the singular suffering of the Jewish people in the concentration camps.

Wiesel had known Walesa since the Polish president's days as leader of the Solidarity movement, and Wiesel was the one who had taken him for his first visit to Auschwitz in the late 1980s. "I wanted to work out the tensions," Wiesel said. "I thought it was wrong to have these tensions risking the sobriety and nobility of the event."

At the last minute, for Wiesel's sake, Walesa made the statement that soothed the situation: "The distance we have walked from the sign that says 'labor liberates' to this death house is symbolic of a journey, a journey down the road that stands for the suffering of many nations, especially the Jewish nation."

When Wiesel received the Nobel Peace Prize in 1986, he used the prize money to launch the Elie Wiesel Foundation for Humanity. His wife, Marion Erster Rose, whom he married in 1969, spends a good deal of her time working for the foundation. She also has helped him by translating his works from French into English. "I respect English too much to write in it," Wiesel once joked.

Among the foundation's activities are international seminars on the "Anatomy of Hate"; an essay contest in which college juniors and seniors examine and analyze ethical issues they confront; the Study and Enrichment Center for children at Hazrot Yassaf, a remote caravan site in the north of Israel at which the children of Israel's forty thousand Ethiopian Jews learn to assimilate into Israeli society; and a second such center in the city of Ashkelon, Beit Tzipora, which is named for Wiesel's sister who was murdered by the Nazis.

Through his work, Wiesel has kept alive the names and the spirits of those hatred would destroy, and in so doing, reemphasized kindness and remembrance. "I've tried to do something with my life to help others do something with theirs. Helping others, that's the main thing. The only way for us to help ourselves is to help others and to listen to each others' stories."

ELIE WIESEL'S TEACHINGS

"With words you can create either angels or demons. Be careful. Do not create demons. Create only angels; create only the good and the humane."

"Beauty without an ethical dimension cannot exist."

"God requires of man not that he live, but that he choose to live. What matters is to choose — at the risk of being defeated."

"Hate is the cancer at the root of human relationships — among individuals and entire nations."

"Man owes it to himself to reject despair."

"To quarrel with God is permissible, even required. One can say anything as long as it is for man, not against him."

"Don't give evil a second chance."

"We are all in the same boat. . . . If we are to survive, we must try to save the world together. That's not easy, but why should it be?"

"You begin with yourself. Our endeavors are limited. We can't affect the multitudes, but we can affect one person here and one person there. Indifference can be stopped in a thousand different ways — mainly by doing what we do and doing it well."

"No one is more capable of gratitude than one who has emerged from death's kingdom. Every moment is a gift of grace."

Oprah Winfrey

The death of Angelica Mena, a four-year-old Chicago girl who had been molested, strangled, and thrown into Lake Michigan by Michael Howarth, who had been convicted twice before of abducting and raping children, set Oprah Winfrey in motion. After she saw the reports on the evening news in mid February, 1991, something snapped. "I didn't know the child, never heard her laughter," Winfrey said. "But I vowed that night to do something, to take a stand for the children of this country."

Winfrey had long been concerned about child victimization. She had learned that experts maintain that abuse victims seek control in their adult lives to compensate for the helplessness they experienced as abused children, tending to abuse children themselves. That she was abused as a child herself, according to that explanation, could account for Winfrey's personal motivation. She'd talked about the issue on her show and sent checks to child advocacy groups.

This time, however, she went to see former Illinois Governor James Thompson, a partner in the prestigious Chicago law firm of Winston & Strawn. Thompson helped her draft child protection legislation for the entire country. "When millions of people look to you to both set an example and to add your voice to theirs, it empowers you to do more than you ordinarily might," the former governor said of Winfrey's fight. "This is a woman with extraordinary commitment."

Winfrey was only thirty-seven in 1991 when she went to Washington, D.C. with her own idea of the law in her hands: The National Child Protection Act, which became known as "the Oprah Bill." The bill required states to register the names and Social Security numbers of and other information about anyone convicted of child molestation and report it to the U.S. Justice Department. That information becomes available through the FBI to employers screening job applicants for positions in which the applicant would have access to children. (At the time, only California, Iowa, Florida, Minnesota, Texas, and Washington had such reporting systems; in one year, these states had discovered sixty-two hundred individuals convicted of serious crimes who sought jobs as child-care providers.)

In Washington, although it is unusual for citizens to prepare legislation themselves, Winfrey won the support of Senator Joseph Biden, chairman of the Senate Judiciary Committee on Child Abuse, who agreed to sponsor the bill, as did Representative Patricia Schroeder. "[Biden] asked for some changes, which we agreed to, and he said 'We'll have hearings in two weeks.' I was stunned," Winfrey reported.

"This is the best proposal that's come before us," Biden told his committee. "The idea is simple: that you must do everything you can to detect the convicted criminal before . . . another tragedy takes place."

At a hearing, Winfrey told the committee, "Everybody deals with their pain differently. Some become overachievers like me, and others become mothers who kill. Pedophiles seek employment where they will be in contact with children," she testified. "There are millions upon millions of silent victims in this country that have been and will continue to be irrevocably harmed unless we do something to stem this horrible tide.

"I wept for Angelica, and I wept for us, a society that apparently cares so little about its children that we would allow a man with two previous convictions for kidnapping and rape of children to go free after serving only seven years of a fifteen-year sentence."

Following the hearing, Winfrey recounted her own experience with child abuse at a press conference. "You lose your childhood when you've been abused. My heart goes out to those children who are abused at home and have no one to turn to."

Her arguments were convincing. Oprah Winfrey enjoyed the satisfaction of personally witnessing President Bill Clinton sign the bill into national law. Clinton said, "Not unlike the Brady Bill, this law creates a national data base network. This one can be used by any child-care provider in America to conduct a background check to determine if a job applicant can be trusted with our children."

With the bill safely on the books, Winfrey now plans to lobby for mandatory sentencing of child abusers. "We have to demonstrate that we value our children enough to say that when you hurt a child, this is what happens to you," Winfrey said. "It is not negotiable."

Winfrey overcame great obstacles in order to be in a position to help so many others. Her background could have come straight from one of her shows. Her parents never married — she was the product of a furlough romance in Mississippi. Soldier Vernon Winfrey, home on leave from the U.S. Army, returned to active duty unaware that nine months later he would be a father. He found out only after Vernita Lee sent him a card announcing their daughter's arrival and asking for baby clothes.

In 1954, work was hard to come by in the small town of Kosciusko, where Winfrey was born, so her mother headed for Milwaukee, Wisconsin, in search of a good-paying job. Winfrey, then a baby, was left in the care of her paternal grandmother, a woman of strong character and religious beliefs who lived by the Bible. Much of Winfrey's early life was spent in church where, by the age of three, she began performing in Christmas and Easter pageants.

To Grandmother Winfrey, performing at church was fine, but at home the youngster was to be seen and not heard. The child rebelled and began acting up. The two were like the immovable object meeting the irresistible force. Her grandmother would not bend, and she would not be controlled.

That was when Winfrey's mother invited her to come and live in Milwaukee. She grabbed the opportunity, but came to learn that rural Mississippi had its advantages over the mean streets of the big city. For one thing, her mother lived in one room, worked long hours, and had little time for a daughter. She had to make do on a welfare check and a maid's wages. There wasn't much left for the extras a child would like — such as going to a movie — so once again, Winfrey turned rebellious.

At twelve, she moved on yet again. This time she lived with her father, Vernon Winfrey, in Nashville, Tennessee. He had a wife by now, and together they put structure in the adolescent's life. Although she could read and write well, she was weak in math and had to study to improve. Her father was as religious as her grandmother, and she found herself again performing at pageants and singing in choruses in church. Oprah Winfrey soon learned she could not wear down these adults as easily as she could her grandmother and mother.

But her mother wanted her back. Her father reluctantly allowed the girl to visit her mother in Milwaukee where her mother convinced the girl things would be better than before. Vernita Lee soon married, and expanded her family with a new son and daughter. But her stepsister had fairer skin, and Winfrey became convinced she was being neglected in favor of this girl because of the difference. At a time when she needed her mother's attention, she felt cast off by everyone at home. She concluded, because of her many moves back and forth between her parents, that neither of them really loved her, and buried herself in her books.

It was during this period that Winfrey became a victim of sexual abuse by male family members and friends. "It happened over a period of years between nine and fourteen," she said. "I remember blaming myself for it, thinking something must be wrong with me." Confused and frightened about this part of her life, she kept the trauma to herself for years. Later, *The Ladies Home Journal* reported that at fourteen, she had given birth to a premature baby who died soon after birth. "Everybody in the family sort of shoved it under a rock," she told the publication. "Because I had been involved in sexual promiscuity, they thought if anything happened, it had to be my fault."

Despite her troubled life, Winfrey continued to be a good student. A teacher helped her get a scholarship to a prestigious school in an affluent area. But her achievements were clouded by emotional outbreaks. On several occasions, Winfrey destroyed family belongings, then pretended their apartment had been burglarized. Twice she ran away. And she was nearly sent to a detention home. Overwhelmed by these events, her mother sent her back to her father.

Back with her father, her life took on purpose and direction. Vernon Winfrey worked hard as a barber and owned a grocery store. He set equally high standards for his daughter's conduct and achievement. "I had to work in the store," she recalls, "and I hated it — every minute of it. Hated it. Selling penny candy, Popsicles. But without him — even with all this potential — I never would have blossomed."

In high school she excelled in public speaking and dramatics. Senior year was an exciting time for her. She attended the 1970 White House Conference on Youth in Washington. On a trip to Los Angeles to speak at a church, she toured Hollywood. A local black radio station in Nashville hired her to read the news. And she became "Miss Black Tennessee."

This recognition helped Winfrey see her own dark skin in a new light. She came to realize it was poise, talent, and intelligence that mattered more than skin color. She won a scholarship to Tennessee State University in Nashville through a speaking contest, and she majored in language arts.

Continuing as a news announcer at WVOL, she was soon hired by a major radio station, WLAC. Before long she made the jump to television at WLAC-TV as a reporter-anchor. Though she was earning five figures, her father still kept her under his thumb with a midnight curfew. To be on her own, she dropped out of college and left Nashville to take a job at WJZ-TV in Baltimore.

There, she found her lack of formal training in broadcast journalism actually worked to her benefit. Her reporting was not objective and she didn't follow direction, preferring to handle stories emotionally. But since she'd signed a solid contract, she couldn't be fired, so management had to find a better use for her talents.

They made her co-host of a local morning show, "People Are Talking," which ran in competition with "Donahue." Suddenly, the subjective quality that had undermined Winfrey's reporting became a strength. She was a stimulating interviewer and her engaging personality was a big hit with audiences. She'd found her niche.

Yet although the five-foot-tall Winfrey was slim, attractive, and earning more than $100,000 per year in Baltimore, old insecurities haunted her. "I had so much going for me, but I still thought I was nothing without a man," she said, referring to her long-term relationship with a boyfriend who eventually rejected her. She had felt depleted and powerless without him. She stayed in bed for three days, missed work, and even attempted suicide.

But she grew from the experience: she came

to realize how she had allowed herself to be abused emotionally. Once she was over the crisis, she was ready to move to the big time in broadcasting. She sent tapes of her show to television stations, landing a job as host on "AM Chicago" at WLS-TV. The ABC affiliate aired its show opposite Phil Donahue, so once again she was competing with the talk-show king.

In no time, Winfrey so overshadowed her competition that the Donahue show retreated to New York. She created such a sensation that "AM Chicago" was renamed "The Oprah Winfrey Show." The move made her the first African-American woman to host her own nationally syndicated show. She is also the first black woman to own a movie-production studio, and after Mary Pickford and Lucille Ball, is only the third female studio owner ever. She has taken leaves of absence from her show to take roles in movies, such as *The Color Purple* and *Native Son*.

In 1986, King World Productions launched the show on national syndication. She eventually bought the show from the parent company, Capital Cities/ABC, and built HARPO Studios (Harpo is Oprah spelled backward.) HARPO Productions is run with Winfrey's own style. "I run this company based on instinct," she said. They must be good instincts because although she has never taken a class in business, hers is the highest-ranked talk show in the history of television. The show is broadcast in most American cities and in fifty-five countries as well.

Winfrey blends earthiness, humor, spontaneity, and candor with a personal touch. "I believe that good communicative television should be a give and take," she says. "You give something to the audience and they give back to you. So I expect my audience and my guests to be as open as I am."

On a program about incest, she impulsively put her arms around the woman speaking and, weeping with her, confided that she too had been sexually abused as a child. "What I have learned in my life and in my work is that the more I am able to be myself, the more it enables other people to be themselves. That is why people tell me things on the air that they have not been able to tell their mother, their daughter, their brother."

Her program shies away from the tawdry and lurid fare of other talk shows — she is most interested in topics that can actually help people improve their lives. These include shows on battered women and alcoholism, building relationships with family members or Attention Deficit Disorder (ADD).

She has been highly successful, and she has

made it a point to share that success with others: She set up scholarships at her alma mater, Tennessee State University, and at Morehouse College; she donated $500,000 to keep the Chicago Academy for the Arts high school open; and she donated $1 million to an inner-city Chicago high school.

She and the women of her staff have also formed a "Big Sister" group with two dozen teenage girls from a Chicago housing project in which drugs and crime are prevalent. Winfrey invites the teens to her place for pajama parties, and takes them to plays and social gatherings. But she also gives them dictionaries with orders to learn five new words a day.

Most of all, she lays down Oprah's law: "Get pregnant and I'll break your face!" She talks to the girls about goals. They say they want Cadillacs. She gives them the facts of life. "If you cannot talk correctly, if you cannot read or do math, if you become pregnant, if you drop out of school, you will never have a Cadillac, I guarantee it! And if you get Ds and Fs on your report card, you're out of this group. Don't tell me you want to do great things in your life if all you carry to school is a radio."

The community-minded Winfrey speaks to numerous youth groups, urging listeners to be achievers. She encourages kids to be everything they can be. And she is determined to help people overcome their own problems.

"I don't think of myself as a poor, deprived ghetto kid who made good," she says. "I think of myself as somebody who from an early age knew I was responsible for myself, and I had to make good."

She has made good indeed, as the country's highest-paid entertainer. "I also believe you create your own blessings," she has said. "You have to prepare yourself so that when the time comes you're ready. She doesn't think success is as difficult as some people make it out to be. It boils down to setting goals and working toward them. And she enjoys that process.

"My main concern about myself is whether I will live up to my potential," she explains. "I still sense that the best is yet to be. . . . The more you praise and celebrate your life, the more there is in life to celebrate. The more you complain, the more you find fault, the more misery and fault you will have to find. I am so glad I did not have to wait until I was fifty-two to figure this out, to understand the law of cause and effect — that divine reciprocity, reaping what you sow, is the absolute truth."

"You only have to believe you can succeed, that you can be whatever your heart desires, be willing to work for it, and you can have it."

"Knowledge is power. With knowledge, you can soar and reach as high as your dreams will take you."

"The more positive you are about your life, the more positive it will be. The more you complain, the more miserable you will be."

"Don't let a bad childhood stand in your way."

"Eat reasonably, diet privately, and exercise regularly."

"Don't be satisfied with just one success — and don't give up after failure."

"Do what you want to do, when you want to do it . . . and not a moment sooner."

"You can't do it all yourself. Don't be afraid to rely on others to help you accomplish your goals."

Appendix

SURVEY OF AMERICAN HEROES

OBJECTIVE: To evaluate various qualities assumed associated with heroism.

SURVEY
METHOD: Telephone

SAMPLING: 800 cross-section interviews The error is ±3.5%.

INTERVIEWING
DATES: January 3–25, 1995

IMPORTANCE RATINGS

Respondents were read a series of issues presumed important to them in considering someone a hero or heroine. For each, they were asked to rate the issue on a scale of

299

"1" to "10" — with "10" having the highest importance, and "1" the lowest. The table that follows shows the percentage of response rating a particular attribute either a "9" or "10."

- "Honesty" was the highest rated attribute (receiving "top two box" mention by 83.4% of the respondents)
- This attribute was followed by . . .
  - "Being compassionate" (71%) and
  - "Having high moral standards" (71%)
- "Being willing to risk your life" was rated 9th of the 18 issues (receiving 54% mention). This attribute issue received the most mentions by . . .
  - respondents in the East South Central region comprising Alabama, Kentucky, Mississippi, and Tennessee (59%)
  - males aged 19–24 (65%)

Importance Ratings — % Top Two Boxes

Being honest	83
Being compassionate	71
Having high moral standards	71
Being determined to overcome obstacles	64
Having strong beliefs	64
Willingness to do right thing	63
Willingness to sacrifice for others	59
Willingness to stand by one's principles	58
Willingness to risk own life	54
Having religious faith	52
Having an optimistic attitude	51
Being persistent	47
Being courageous	42
Being modest	36
Being resilient	24
Being physically gifted	14
Being famous	6

Teenagers were asked to rate the same issues as were the random sample. Teenagers put "honesty" at the top of their list (83%), but . . .

- They put "being determined to overcome obstacles" in second place (66%) and
- "being willing to do the right thing" in third place (64%)

Importance Ratings —
Teenagers % Top Two Boxes

Being honest	83
Being compassionate	61
Having high moral standards	49
Being determined to overcome obstacles	66
Having strong beliefs	53
Willingness to do right thing	64
Willingness to sacrifice for others	57
Willingness to stand by one's principles	59
Willingness to risk own life	53
Having religious faith	39
Having an optimistic attitude	44
Being persistent	41
Being courageous	36
Being modest	37
Being resilient	25
Being physically gifted	15
Being famous	8

0   20   40   60   80   100

Teenagers also rated the following attributes lower than did the random sample:

- "Being compassionate"

- "Having high moral standards"

- "Having strong beliefs"

- "Having religious faith"

Teenage boys rated the attribute of "being determined to overcome obstacles" higher than did girls (72% for boys versus 62% for girls), but girls rated the following issues higher than boys:

- "Being honest"

- "Willingness to stand by one's principles"

- "Having high moral standards"

- "Being compassionate" (by a wide margin)

- "Having an optimistic attitude"

- "Having strong beliefs"

Comparison of Random Sample
with Teenager Sample

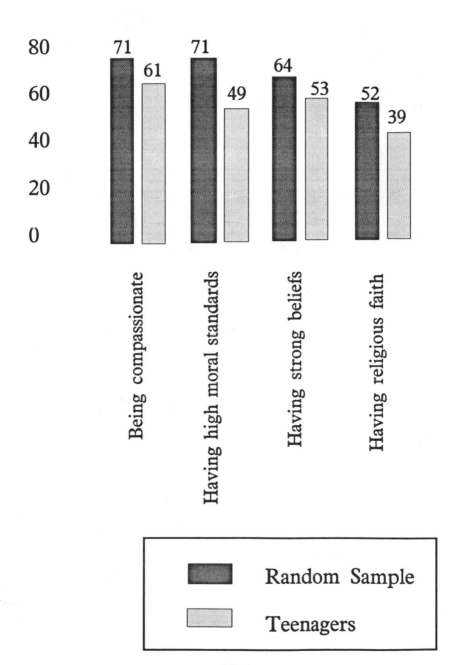

Teenagers: Male versus Female

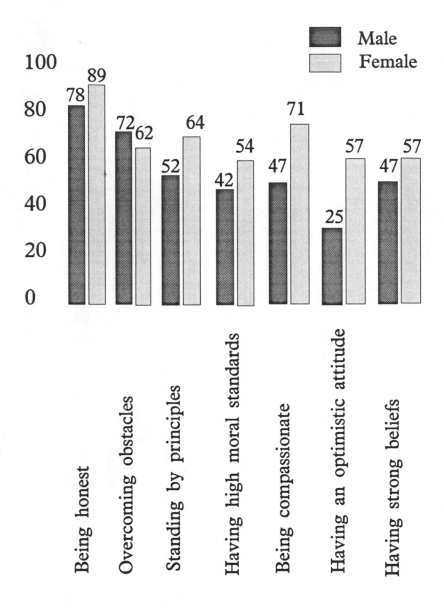

Qualities That Would Disqualify a Person from Heroic Status

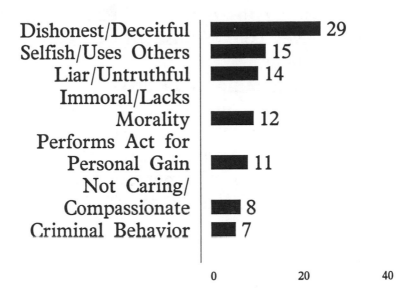

Dishonest/Deceitful	29
Selfish/Uses Others	15
Liar/Untruthful	14
Immoral/Lacks Morality	12
Performs Act for Personal Gain	11
Not Caring/Compassionate	8
Criminal Behavior	7

0   20   40

Importance Attributes

The following is the full wording of the attributes asked about.

Being honest
Being modest
Being courageous
Being determined to overcome obstacles
Being persistent
Having religious faith
Being physically gifted
Being resilient

Being willing to sacrifice themselves for
the sake of others
Being willing to risk their lives
Being willing to stand by their principles
and never compromise them
Being famous
Having high moral standards
Being always willing to do the right thing
regardless of the consequences
Being compassionate toward others
Having an optimistic mental attitude
Having strong beliefs that guide their
lives

AGREEMENT STATEMENTS

The following is the full wording of the agreement statements:

It is important to have a spiritual life.
There are circumstances where lying
is OK.
Marriage is a dying institution.
Under certain circumstances, violence
is appropriate.
A true hero never gives up. They bounce
back and overcome adversity.
There are fewer heroes and heroines
today than there were ten years ago.

There will be fewer heroes and heroines ten years from now than there are today.

The media make heroes and heroines out of people who really don't deserve it.

We need more heroes and heroines.

Heroism really isn't any one act. It's an everyday way of living.

America doesn't show its heroes and heroines enough appreciation.

Anyone can be a hero. It's just a matter of being in the right place at the right time.

Athletic skills shouldn't make a person a hero or heroine.

Once a person receives heroic status they can't lose it.

Also of special interest was . . .

- 4 out of 5 (80%) saying, "We need more heroes and heroines." This belief being most strongly held by . . .

- Those in the West Central Region comprising Arkansas, Louisiana, Oklahoma, and Texas (84%) and

- Females, aged 25-34 (87%)

- Almost 2 out of 5 (39%) believed "marriage is a dying institution." Sadly, this feeling was most promiment among younger respondents (i.e. aged 19-24).

- More than 1 of 3 (35%) felt violence is appropriate in certain circumstances. This was felt most strongly by men aged 25-49.

- And almost 1 of 3 (31%) felt it was acceptable to lie under certain circumstances. Men, especially younger men and senior men, agreed most frequently with this position, while senior females especially disagreed with it.

Agreement Statements (% "Agree")

Statement	% Agree
Spiritual life important	87
Heroism everyday way of living	84
If you've ever done anything bad . . .	85
True hero never gives up	84
Media makes undeserving heroes	84
We need more heroes	80
Athletic skills shouldn't make a person a hero	77
America doesn't appreciate its heroes	73
Anyone can be a hero	52
Fewer heroes today	50
There will be fewer heroes in ten years	41
Marriage is a dying institution	39
Violence is sometimes appropriate	35
Lying is OK sometimes	31
Heroic status can't be lost	15

0 20 40 60 80 100

311

Teenagers were read the same series of statements and also asked if they "agreed" or "disagreed" with each.

Teenagers — in fact 9 out of 10 — put needing more heroes and heroines at the top of their list. This was felt equally strongly by teenage boys and girls. This response was closely followed by . . .

- 89% who felt a "true hero never gives up" — which was slightly more than the cross-section, and

- 85% who areed that one can still be considered a hero or heroine if they've ever done "anything bad" — which was the same proportion as the cross-section.

Agreement Statements — Teenagers
(% "Agree")

Statement	%
Spiritual life important	73
Heroism everyday way of living	89
If you've ever done anything bad . . .	85
True hero never gives up	89
Media makes undeserving heroes	70
We need more heroes	90
Athletic skills shouldn't make a person a hero	78
America doesn't appreciate its heroes	70
Anyone can be a hero	56
Fewer heroes today	48
There will be fewer heroes in ten years	43
Marriage is a dying institution	43
Violence is sometimes appropriate	42
Lying is OK sometimes	46
Heroic status can't be lost	17

0   20   40   60   80   100

While teenagers more strongly agreed than their older counterparts that we need more heroes and heroines, they also were . . .

- more likely to feel lying is acceptable under certain circumstances
- less likely to consider a spiritual life important, and
- less likely to think the media makes heroes out of people who don't deserve it.

Agreement Statements Comparison of Random Sample with Teenagers

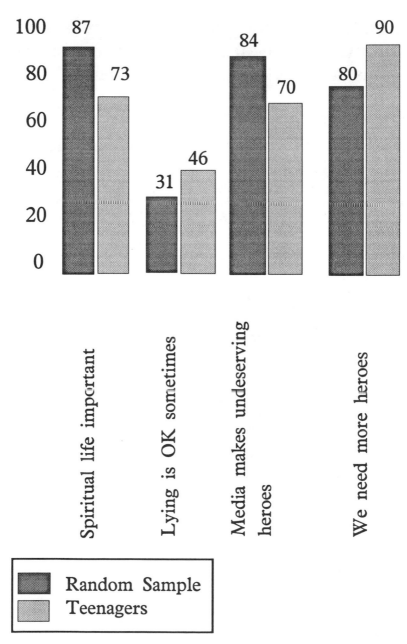

There was one significant difference in response between teenage boys and girls on the agreement statements. Specifically . . .

- significantly more boys than girls agreed with the statement that "under certain circumstances, violence is appropriate."

AGREE
"Under certain circumstances, violence is appropriate."

Teenage Boys versus Teenage Girls

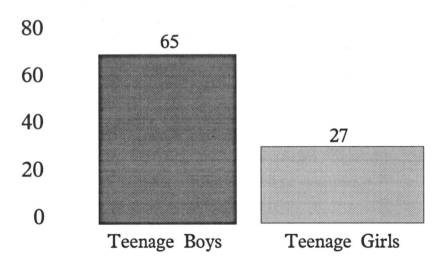

Teenage boys hold the highest level of agreement with this statement.

Agreement of males by age that . . . "Under certain circumstances, violence is appropriate."

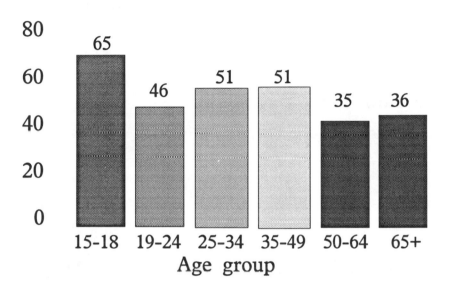

Age group

HYPOTIIETICAL QUESTIONS

HYPOTHETICAL SITUATION

If you found a wallet in the street with $5,000 in it, would you turn it in?

Of the random sample:

- 1 in 10 said they wouldn't turn in the wallet
- 86% said they would
- 4% didn't know

Of the teenagers:

- 75% answered yes

But, even among the cross-section . . .

- Younger respondents said they'd be less likely to turn the wallet in than did older respondents

Would Turn Wallet In By Age

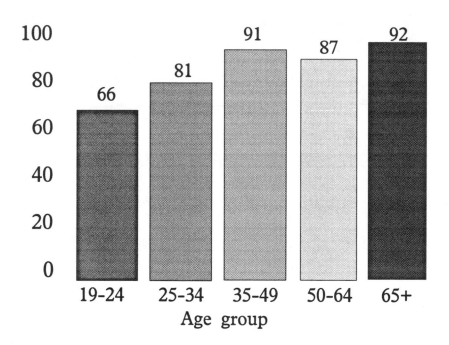

HYPOTHETICAL SITUATION

If you banged someone's car in a parking lot — but no one saw you — would you turn yourself in?

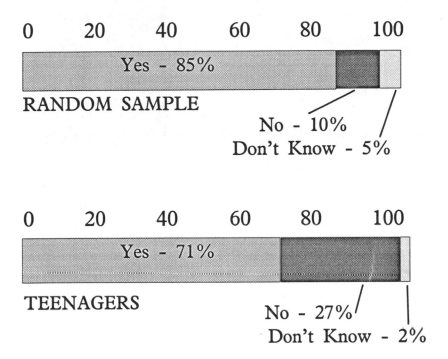

0   20   40   60   80   100

Yes - 85%

RANDOM SAMPLE

No - 10%

Don't Know - 5%

0   20   40   60   80   100

Yes - 71%

TEENAGERS

No - 27%

Don't Know - 2%

Would Turn Themselves in if Banged Car By Age

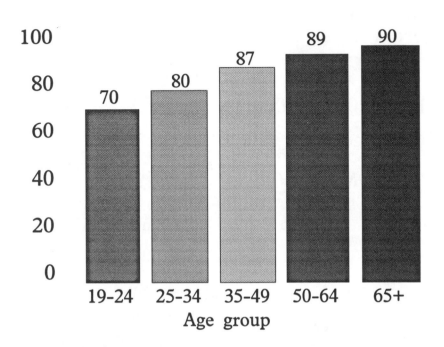

HYPOTHETICAL SITUATION

Would you be unfaithful if you knew you wouldn't get caught? Of the random sample:

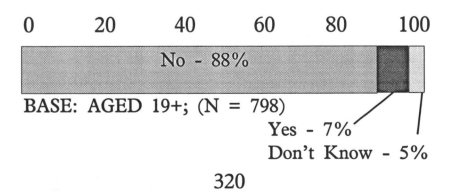

Would Be Unfaithful if Knew Wouldn't Get Caught By Income

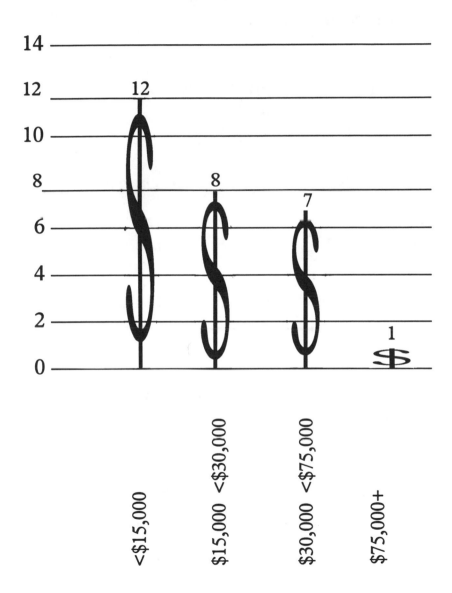

Among the cross-section, there was really no difference in response by sex with respect to this hypothetical situation. Men and women — in equal proportions — said they would be unfaithful.

Would Be Unfaithful if Knew
Wouldn't Get Caught
By Gender (answering yes)

Gender	percentage
Male	7
Female	7

Those cross-section respondents who were 19–49 years of age were asked the following question:

If you knew one of your parents were cheating, would you tell the other parent?

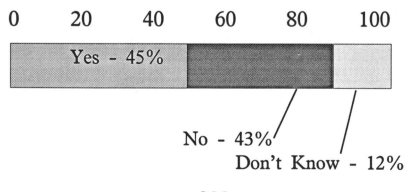

322

The response to this question was split —
with 45% saying they would tell the other
parent, and 43% saying they wouldn't.

There was no difference in response to
the "parents cheating" question by gender,
educational attainment, or income. But the
younger a respondent was, the more likely
he or she would be to tell the other parent.

Would Tell the Other Parent By Age

Age	percentage
19-24	64
25-34	50
35-49	39

HYPOTHETICAL SITUATION

If you knew one of your close relations
were cheating, would you tell his or her
spouse?

Of the random sample:
- 22% said yes
- 62% said no
- 17% didn't know

NOTE: Asked of respondents aged 49
and older. N = 239

If Relation Cheating, Would Tell Spouse By Educational Attainment

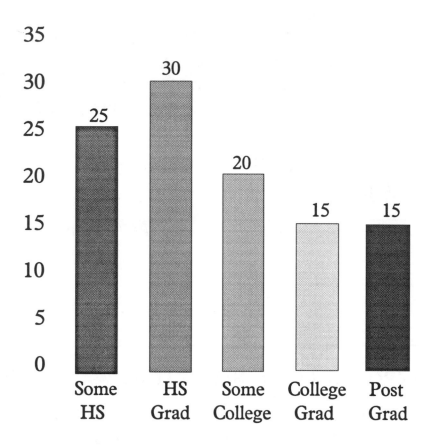

HYPOTHETICAL SITUATION

If your best friend were doing something illegal, would you turn him or her in?
Of the random sample:
- 41% said yes
- 42% said no
- 17% didn't know

60% of teenagers (aged 15–18) said they would not turn in their friend for doing something illegal. This contrasts with the random sample cross-section wherein 42% said they wouldn't.

Moreover, teenagers seem less undecided about what they'd do. Only 7% of teenagers said they didn't know what they'd do if faced with that situation, but 17% of those aged 19 and over said they didn't know what they'd do.

When asked if they would cheat on a school test if they would get a better grade and not get caught, teenagers answered in the following manner . . .

- 40% said they would
- 59% said they wouldn't (with only 1% not sure of what they'd do)

Slightly more boys than girls said they'd cheat on a test (45% for boys and 37% for girls).

HYPOTHETICAL SITUATION

If your friends wanted you to do something that you knew was wrong — but it made you popular — would you do it?

All teenaged respondents were asked this question. The response was . . .

0	20	40	60	80	100

No - 89%

Yes - 9%
Don't Know - 2%

SURVEY CALLING SCRIPT EXCERPTS

Hello, my name is _____, and I'm calling from TMR, Inc., a national marketing research company. We're conducting a study and would like to ask you a few brief questions.

(ASK TO SPEAK TO MALE IN HOUSEHOLD 15 YEARS OF AGE OR OLDER)

Are you 15 years of age or older? (IF NOT, ASK TO SPEAK TO SOMEONE WHO IS)

30. For classification purposes only, would you please tell me your age?

Are you . . . (READ CHOICES)
- 18 to 24
- 25 to 34
- 35 to 49
- 50 to 64
- 65 or over
- (DO NOT READ) Refused
- 15 to 17

30A. Are you . . .
- 18 years old
- 19 years old
- 20 to 24 years old

70. This portion of our survey is concerned with heroes and heroines — and particularly those who are currently alive. I'm going to read you a number of qualities that some people consider important for someone to be considered a hero or heroine. As I read each quality, and using a scale from one to ten, please tell me how important you consider that quality to be. If you think the quality is extremely important, you would give it a ten. If you think it's not at all important to being considered a hero or heroine, you would give it a one. If you think it's anywhere in

between a one and a ten, you would give it whatever number you consider appropriate. Let's start with (READ ITEM).
How important do you feel this quality is for being considered heroic?

10 = EXTREMELY IMPORTANT =====>
1 = NOT AT ALL IMPORTANT

- Being honest
- Being modest
- Being courageous
- Being determined to overcome obstacles
- Being persistent
- Having religious faith
- Being physically gifted
- Being resilient
- Being willing to sacrifice themselves for the sake of others
- Being willing to risk their lives
- Being willing to stand by their principles and never compromise them
- Being famous
- Having high moral standards
- Being always willing to do the right thing regardless of the consequences
- Being compassionate toward others
- Having an optimistic mental attitude
- Having strong beliefs that guide their lives

71. In your opinion, what would disqualify a person from being considered a hero or heroine?

INTERVIEWER: RECORD RESPONSE ON VBA SHEET. PROBE FOR CLARITY AND COMPLETENESS

- SELECT THIS TO CONTINUE

72. I'm going to read you a number of statements. As I read each one, please tell me if you agree or disagree with it. Let's start with (READ ITEM) . . .

1 = AGREE; 2 = DISAGREE; 9 = DON'T KNOW

- It's important to have a spiritual life.
- There are circumstances where lying is OK.
- Marriage is a dying institution.
- Under certain circumstances, violence is appropriate.
- A true hero never gives up. They bounce back and overcome adversity.
- There are fewer heroes and heroines today than there were ten years ago.
- There will be fewer heroes and heroines ten years from now than there are today.

- The media makes heroes and heroines out of people who really don't deserve it.
- We need more heroes and heroines.
- Heroism really isn't any one act. It's an everyday way of living.
- America doesn't show its heroes and heroines enough appreciation.
- Anyone can be a hero. It's just a matter of being in the right place at the right time.
- Athletic skills shouldn't make a person a hero or heroine.
- Once a person receives heroic status they can't lose it.

73. I'm going to read you a number of hypothetical situations. As I read each one, please answer yes or no.

1 = YES; 2 = NO; 9 = DON'T KNOW

- If you found a wallet in the street with $5,000 in it, would you turn it in?
- Would you cheat on a school test if you knew you wouldn't get caught and knew you'd get a better grade?
- If you knew one of your parents were cheating, would you tell your other parent?

- If you knew one of your close relations were cheating, would you tell his or her spouse?
- If your best friend were doing something illegal, would you turn him or her in?
- If you banged someone's car in a parking lot — but no one saw you — would you turn yourself in?
- If your friends wanted you to do something that you knew was wrong — but it made you popular — would you do it?
- Would you be unfaithful if you knew you wouldn't get caught?

32A. Are you . . .
- married
- single
- divorced
- widowed
- separated
- (DO NOT READ) Refused

32B. What is your religion? Are you . . .
- Protestant
- Catholic
- Jewish
- Muslim
- Budhist

331

- some other religion
- (DO NOT READ) Refused
- ??

32C. Thinking over the past week, approximately how many hours have you spent reading a book?
- Number of hours

37. It is possible we may want to talk to you in more depth. If so, would it be OK if we called you to talk some more?
- Yes
- No

31. Would you consider yourself to be . . . (READ CHOICES)
- White
- Black
- Hispanic
- some other race
- (DO NOT READ) Refused

32. What is the highest level of education you have completed? (DO NOT READ CHOICES)
- some high school
- graduated high school
- some college
- graduated college
- postgraduate
- (DO NOT READ) Refused

36. Finally, which of these categories best fits your total household income for the past year? (READ CHOICES)
- under $15,000
- $15,000 to $19,999
- $20,000 to $29,999
- $30,000 to $39,999
- $40,000 to $49,999
- $50,000 to $74,999
- $75,000 to $99,999
- $100,000 or more
- (DO NOT READ) Refused
- (DO NOT READ) Don't know

SEX. INTERVIEWER, RECORD SEX OF RESPONDENT FROM VOICE. DO NOT ASK.
- male
- female

RESPINFO. INTERVIEWER, RECORD RESPONDENT INFORMATION BELOW:
- ! name
- ! street address 1
- ! street address 2
- ! city
- ! state
- ! ZIP

About the Authors

DR. ROBERT PAMPLIN has experienced incredible financial success. As an undergraduate in the 1960s, he caught the rise of the stock market, making his first million. He later invested those profits in timber and farmlands, just before they shot up in value. And his $30,000 investment in an unproven "cutting" horse led to $2 million in stud fees, and the horse's eventual sale for $850,000.

His lifelong tutor has been his father. Together they run a family company that owns nineteen textile miles as well as a concrete and asphalt company. R.B. Pamplin Corporation sales in 1995 were $800 million.

Dr. Pamplin has also authored twelve books and earned eight degrees. He has served as chairman of both Lewis and Clark College and the University of Portland. He's been awarded many honorary degrees and has served on state and presidential commissions. The *Forbes 400* member resides near Portland, Oregon.

GARY K. EISLER is an award-winning writer whose work has appeared in publications such as *Forbes* and *The Wall Street Journal.* He has published and edited newspapers and magazines and has worked in public relations. He also is a small woodland owner and a producer of spring water. He has been married for twenty-eight years and is the father of three children.

The employees of THORNDIKE PRESS hope you have enjoyed this Large Print book. All our Large Print books are designed for easy reading — and they're made to last.

Other Thorndike Large Print books are available at your library, through selected bookstores, or directly from us. Suggestions for books you would like to see in Large Print are always welcome.

For more information about current and upcoming titles, please call or mail your name and address to:

THORNDIKE PRESS
PO Box 159
Thorndike, Maine 04986
800/223-6121
207/948-2962